ABOUT THIS PUBLICATION

FOR SERVICE ASSISTANCE

Customer Service Department
704.898.0770

www.visionbooks.org

TID: 5015339
ISBN (10) digit: 1502485362
ISBN (13) digit: 978-1502485366

123-4-56789-01234-Paperback
123-4-56789-01234-Hardback

First Edition

090520140547

Printed in the United States of America

1

2015 EDITION

North Carolina Criminal Law

And Procedure-Pamphlet # 17

Printed In conjunction with the Administration of the Courts

North Carolina Criminal Law and Procedure
Pamphlet Reference Guide

7

8

9

10

11

13

Chapter 21

Bills of Lading.

Article 1.

Definitions.

§§ 21-1 through 21-3. Repealed by Session Laws 1965, c. 700, s. 2.

Article 2.

Issue of Bills of Lading.

§§ 21-4 through 21-8. Repealed by Session Laws 1965, c. 700, s. 2.

Article 3.

Obligations and Rights of Carriers upon Bills of Lading.

§§ 21-9 through 21-27: Repealed by Session Laws 1965, c. 700, s. 2.

Article 4.

Negotiation and Transfer of Bills.

§§ 21-28 through 21-41: Repealed by Session Laws 1965, c. 700, s. 2.

Article 5.

Criminal Offenses.

§ 21-42. Issuing false bills or violating Chapter made felony.

Any person who, knowingly or with intent to defraud, falsely makes, alters, forges, counterfeits, prints or photographs any bill of lading purporting to represent goods received for shipment in this State, or with intent utters or

15

publishes as true and genuine any such falsely altered, forged, counterfeited, falsely printed or photographed bill of lading, knowing it to be falsely altered, forged, counterfeited, falsely printed or photographed, or aids in making, altering, forging, counterfeiting, printing, or photographing, or uttering or publishing the same, or issues or aids in issuing or procuring the issue of, or negotiates or transfers for value a bill which contains a false statement as to the receipt of the goods, or as to any other matter, or who, with intent to defraud, violates or fails to comply with, or aids in any violation of, or failure to comply with any provision of this Chapter, shall be guilty of a Class I felony. (1919, c. 65, s. 41; c. 290; C.S., s. 323; 1979, 2nd Sess., c. 1316, s. 23; 1981, c. 63; c. 179.)

Chapter 22.

Contracts Requiring Writing.

§ 22-1. Contracts charging representative personally; promise to answer for debt of another.

No action shall be brought whereby to charge an executor, administrator or collector upon a special promise to answer damages out of his own estate or to charge any defendant upon a special promise to answer the debt, default or miscarriage of another person, unless the agreement upon which such action shall be brought, or some memorandum or note thereof, shall be in writing, and signed by the party charged therewith or some other person thereunto by him lawfully authorized. (29 Charles II, c. 3, s. 4; 1826, c. 10; R.C., c. 50, s. 15; Code, s. 1552; Rev., s. 974; C.S., s. 987.)

§ 22-2. Contract for sale of land; leases.

All contracts to sell or convey any lands, tenements or hereditaments, or any interest in or concerning them, and all leases and contracts for leasing land for the purpose of digging for gold or other minerals, or for mining generally, of whatever duration; and all other leases and contracts for leasing lands exceeding in duration three years from the making thereof, shall be void unless said contract, or some memorandum or note thereof, be put in writing and signed by the party to be charged therewith, or by some other person by him thereto lawfully authorized. (29 Charles II, c. 3, ss. 1, 2, 3; 1819, c. 1016, P.R.;

1844, c. 44; R.C., c. 50, s. 11; 1868, c. 156, ss. 2, 33; Code, ss. 1554, 1743; Rev., s. 976; C.S., s. 988.)

§ 22-3: Repealed by Session Laws 1995, c. 379, s. 15.

§ 22-4. Promise to revive debt of bankrupt.

No promise to pay a debt discharged by any decree of a court of competent jurisdiction, in any proceeding in bankruptcy, shall be received in evidence unless such promise is in writing and signed by the party to be charged therewith. (1899, c. 57; Rev., s. 978; C.S., s. 990.)

§ 22-5. Commercial loan commitments.

No commercial loan commitment by a bank, savings and loan association, or credit union for a loan in excess of fifty thousand dollars ($50,000) shall be binding unless the commitment is in writing and signed by the party to be bound. As used in this section, the term "commercial loan commitment" means an offer, agreement, commitment, or contract to extend credit primarily for business or commercial purposes and does not include charge or credit card accounts, personal lines of credit, overdrafts, or any other consumer account. Offers, agreements, commitments, or contracts to extend credit primarily for aquaculture, agricultural, or farming purposes are specifically exempted from the provisions of this section. (1989, c. 678.)

Chapter 22A.

Signatures.

§ 22A-1. Use of a signature facsimile by a person with a disability.

A person with a disability, as defined in G.S. 168A-3(7a), may use a registered signature facsimile as a proper mark of the person's legal signature. An example of the signature facsimile shall be registered by the person with a disability with the clerk of the superior court in the county where the person lives. The registered signature facsimile may be revoked at any time in writing by the person with a disability. (1973, c. 878; 1997-208, s. 1; 2009-570, s. 34.)

Chapter 22B.

Contracts Against Public Policy.

Article 1.

Invalid Agreements.

§ 22B-1. Construction indemnity agreements invalid.

Any promise or agreement in, or in connection with, a contract or agreement relative to the design, planning, construction, alteration, repair or maintenance of a building, structure, highway, road, appurtenance or appliance, including moving, demolition and excavating connected therewith, purporting to indemnify or hold harmless the promisee, the promisee's independent contractors, agents, employees, or indemnitees against liability for damages arising out of bodily injury to persons or damage to property proximately caused by or resulting from the negligence, in whole or in part, of the promisee, its independent contractors, agents, employees, or indemnitees, is against public policy and is void and unenforceable. Nothing contained in this section shall prevent or prohibit a contract, promise or agreement whereby a promisor shall indemnify or hold harmless any promisee or the promisee's independent contractors, agents, employees or indemnitees against liability for damages resulting from the sole negligence of the promisor, its agents or employees. This section shall not affect an insurance contract, workers' compensation, or any other agreement issued by an insurer, nor shall this section apply to promises or agreements under which a public utility as defined in G.S. 62-3(23) including a railroad corporation as an indemnitee. This section shall not apply to contracts entered into by the Department of Transportation pursuant to G.S. 136-28.1. (1979, c. 597, s. 1; 1991, c. 636, s. 3; 1993, c. 553, s. 12.)

§ 22B-2. Contracts to improve real property.

A provision in any contract, subcontract, or purchase order for the improvement of real property in this State, or the providing of materials therefor, is void and against public policy if it makes the contract, subcontract, or purchase order

18

subject to the laws of another state, or provides that the exclusive forum for any litigation, arbitration, or other dispute resolution process is located in another state. (1993, c. 294, s. 2.)

§ 22B-3. Contracts with forum selection provisions.

Except as otherwise provided in this section, any provision in a contract entered into in North Carolina that requires the prosecution of any action or the arbitration of any dispute that arises from the contract to be instituted or heard in another state is against public policy and is void and unenforceable. This prohibition shall not apply to non-consumer loan transactions or to any action or arbitration of a dispute that is commenced in another state pursuant to a forum selection provision with the consent of all parties to the contract at the time that the dispute arises. (1993, c. 436, s. 2; 1995, c. 100, s. 1.)

§ 22B-4. Prohibition on contract provisions restricting whistle-blowing related to State Health Plan.

A provision in any contract is void and against public policy if it prohibits an employee's or contractor's ability to report wrongdoing under G.S. 135-48.15 related to the State Health Plan. (2012-192, s. 2.)

§ 22B-5. Reserved for future codification purposes.

§ 22B-6. Reserved for future codification purposes.

§ 22B-7. Reserved for future codification purposes.

§ 22B-8. Reserved for future codification purposes.

§ 22B-9. Reserved for future codification purposes.

Article 2.

Jury Trial Waivers Unenforceable.

§ 22B-10. Contract provisions waiving jury trial unenforceable.

Any provision in a contract requiring a party to the contract to waive his right to a jury trial is unconscionable as a matter of law and the provision shall be unenforceable. This section does not prohibit parties from entering into agreements to arbitrate or engage in other forms of alternative dispute resolution. (1993, c. 463, s. 5; 1993 (Reg. Sess., 1994), c. 763, s. 2.)

§ 22B-11: Reserved for future codification purposes.

§ 22B-12: Reserved for future codification purposes.

§ 22B-13: Reserved for future codification purposes.

§ 22B-14: Reserved for future codification purposes.

§ 22B-15: Reserved for future codification purposes.

§ 22B-16: Reserved for future codification purposes.

§ 22B-17: Reserved for future codification purposes.

§ 22B-18: Reserved for future codification purposes.

§ 22B-19: Reserved for future codification purposes.

Article 3.

Deed Restrictions, Covenants, and Other Agreements Prohibiting Solar Collectors.

§ 22B-20. Deed restrictions and other agreements prohibiting solar collectors.

(a)   The intent of the General Assembly is to protect the public health, safety, and welfare by encouraging the development and use of solar resources and by prohibiting deed restrictions, covenants, and other similar agreements that could have the ultimate effect of driving the costs of owning and maintaining a residence beyond the financial means of most owners.

(b)   Except as provided in subsection (d) of this section, any deed restriction, covenant, or similar binding agreement that runs with the land that would prohibit, or have the effect of prohibiting, the installation of a solar collector that gathers solar radiation as a substitute for traditional energy for water heating, active space heating and cooling, passive heating, or generating electricity for a residential property on land subject to the deed restriction, covenant, or agreement is void and unenforceable. As used in this section, the term "residential property" means property where the predominant use is for residential purposes. The term "residential property" does not include any condominium created under Chapter 47A or 47C of the General Statutes located in a multi-story building containing units having horizontal boundaries described in the declaration. As used in this section, the term "declaration" has the same meaning as in G.S. 47A-3 or G.S. 47C-1-103, depending on the chapter of the General Statutes under which the condominium was created.

(c)   This section does not prohibit a deed restriction, covenant, or similar binding agreement that runs with the land that would regulate the location or screening of solar collectors as described in subsection (b) of this section, provided the deed restriction, covenant, or similar binding agreement does not have the effect of preventing the reasonable use of a solar collector for a residential property. If an owners' association is responsible for exterior maintenance of a structure containing individual residences, a deed restriction, covenant, or similar binding agreement that runs with the land may provide that (i) the title owner of the residence shall be responsible for all damages caused by the installation, existence, or removal of solar collectors; (ii) the title owner of the residence shall hold harmless and indemnify the owners' association for any damages caused by the installation, existence, or removal of solar collectors; and (iii) the owners' association shall not be responsible for maintenance, repair, replacement, or removal of solar collectors unless expressly agreed in a written agreement that is recorded in the office of the register of deeds in the county or counties in which the property is situated. As used in this section, "owners' association" has the same meaning as in G.S. 47F-1-103.

(d)   This section does not prohibit a deed restriction, covenant, or similar binding agreement that runs with the land that would prohibit the location of solar collectors as described in subsection (b) of this section that are visible by a person on the ground:

(1)   On the facade of a structure that faces areas open to common or public access;

(2)   On a roof surface that slopes downward toward the same areas open to common or public access that the façade of the structure faces; or

(3)   Within the area set off by a line running across the façade of the structure extending to the property boundaries on either side of the façade, and those areas of common or public access faced by the structure.

(e)   In any civil action arising under this section, the court may award costs and reasonable attorneys' fees to the prevailing party. (2007-279, s. 3; 2009-553, s. 3.)

Chapter 22C

Payments to Subcontractors.

§ 22C-1. Definitions.

Unless the context otherwise requires in this Chapter:

(1)   "Contractor" means a person who contracts with an owner to improve real property.

(2)   "Improve" means to build, effect, alter, repair, or demolish any improvement upon, connected with, or on or beneath the surface of any real property, or to excavate, clear, grade, fill or landscape any real property, or to construct driveways and private roadways, or to furnish materials, including trees and shrubbery, for any of such purposes, or to perform any labor upon such improvements, and shall also mean and include any design or other professional or skilled services furnished by architects, engineers, land surveyors and landscape architects registered under Chapters 83A, 89C or 89A of the General Statutes.

(3)   "Improvement" means all or any part of any building, structure, erection, alteration, demolition, excavation, clearing, grading, filling, or landscaping, including trees and shrubbery, driveways, and private roadways, on real property.

(4)   An "owner" is a person who has an interest in the real property improved and for whom an improvement is made and who ordered the improvement to be made. "Owner" includes successors in interest of the owner and agents of the owner acting within their authority.

(5)   "Real property" means the real estate that is improved, including lands, leaseholds, tenements and hereditaments, and improvements placed thereon.

(6)   "Subcontractor" means any person who has contracted to furnish labor or materials to, or has performed labor for, a contractor or another subcontractor in connection with a contract to improve real property. (1987 (Reg. Sess., 1988), c. 946, s. 1.)

23

§ 22C-2. Performance by subcontractor.

Performance by a subcontractor in accordance with the provisions of its contract shall entitle it to payment from the party with whom it contracts. Payment by the owner to a contractor is not a condition precedent for payment to a subcontractor and payment by a contractor to a subcontractor is not a condition precedent for payment to any other subcontractor, and an agreement to the contrary is unenforceable. (1987 (Reg. Sess., 1988), c. 946; 1991, c. 620.)

§ 22C-3. Time of payment to subcontractors after contractor or other subcontractor has been paid.

When a subcontractor has performed in accordance with the provisions of his contract, the contractor shall pay to his subcontractor and each subcontractor shall pay to his subcontractor, within seven days of receipt by the contractor or subcontractor of each periodic or final payment, the full amount received for such subcontractor's work and materials based on work completed or service provided under the subcontract. (1987 (Reg. Sess., 1988), c. 946.)

§ 22C-4. Conditions of payment.

Nothing in this Chapter shall prevent the contractor, at the time of application and certification to the owner, from withholding such application and certification to the owner for payment to the subcontractor for: unsatisfactory job progress; defective construction not remedied; disputed work; third party claims filed or reasonable evidence that claim will be filed; failure of subcontractor to make timely payments for labor, equipment, and materials; damage to contractor or another subcontractor; reasonable evidence that subcontract cannot be completed for the unpaid balance of the subcontract sum; or a reasonable amount for retainage not to exceed the initial percentage retained by the owner. (1987 (Reg. Sess., 1988), c. 946.)

§ 22C-5. Late payments to bear interest.

24

Should any periodic or final payment to a subcontractor be delayed by more than seven days after receipt of periodic or final payment by the contractor or subcontractor, the contractor or subcontractor shall pay his subcontractor interest, beginning on the eighth day, at the rate of one percent (1%) per month or a fraction thereof on such unpaid balance as may be due. (1987 (Reg. Sess., 1988), c. 946.)

§ 22C-6. Applicability of this Chapter.

The provisions of this Chapter shall not be applicable to residential contractors as defined in G.S. 87 10(1a), or to improvements to real property intended for residential purposes which are exempted from the application of Chapter 83A of the General Statutes pursuant to G.S. 83A-13(c)(1), or to improvements to real property intended for residential purposes which consist of 12 or fewer residential units. (1987 (Reg. Sess., 1988), c. 946.)

Chapter 23

Debtor and Creditor.

Article 1.

Assignments for Benefit of Creditors.

§ 23-1. Debts mature on execution of assignment; no preferences.

Upon the execution of any voluntary deed of trust or deed of assignment for the benefit of creditors, all debts of the maker thereof shall become due and payable at once, and no such deed of trust or deed of assignment shall contain any preferences of one creditor over another, except as hereinafter stated. (1893, c. 453; Rev., s. 967; 1909, c. 918, s. 1; C.S., s. 1609.)

§ 23-2. Trustee to file schedule of property.

Upon the execution of such deed of trust, the trustee, whether named therein or appointed as hereafter provided for, shall file with the clerk of the superior court of the county in which said deed of trust is registered, within ten days after the registration thereof, an inventory under oath, giving a complete, full and perfect account of all property that has come into his hands or to the hands of any person for him, by virtue of such deed of trust, and when further property of any kind not included in any previous return comes to the hands or knowledge of such trustee he shall return the same as hereinbefore prescribed within ten days after the possession or discovery thereof. (1893, c. 453, s. 2; Rev., s. 968; C.S., s. 1610.)

§ 23-3. Trustee to recover property conveyed fraudulently or in preference.

It is the duty of the trustee to recover, for the benefit of the estate, property which was conveyed by the grantor or assignor in fraud of his creditors, or which was conveyed or transferred by the grantor or assignor for the purpose of giving a preference. A preference, under this section, shall be deemed to have been given when property has been transferred or conveyed within four months next preceding the registration of the deed of trust or deed of assignment in consideration of the payment of a pre-existing debt, when the grantee or transferee of such property knows or has reasonable ground to believe that the grantor or assignor was insolvent at the time of making such conveyance or transfer. (1909, c. 918, s. 2; C.S., s. 1611.)

§ 23-4. Substitute for incompetent trustee appointed in special proceeding.

When a trustee named in a deed of assignment for the benefit of creditors has died or resigned or has in any way become incompetent to execute the trust, the clerk of the superior court of the county wherein said deed of assignment has been registered is authorized and empowered, in a special proceeding in which all persons interested have been made parties, to appoint some discreet and competent person to act as such trustee and to execute all the trusts created in the original deed of assignment, according to its true intent and as fully as if originally appointed trustee therein. (1915, c. 176, s. 1; C.S., s. 1612.)

§ 23-5. Insolvent trustee removed unless bond given; substitute appointed.

26

Upon the complaint of any creditor of the assignor or trustee in such deed of trust, alleging under oath that the trustee named therein is insolvent, and asking that he be required to give bond or be removed, it is the duty of the clerk of the superior court of the county in which such deed of trust is registered, upon a notice of not more than ten days to such trustee, to hear the complaint. If upon such hearing the clerk is satisfied that such trustee is insolvent, he shall remove such trustee and appoint some competent person to execute the provisions of such deed of trust, unless such insolvent trustee shall file with the clerk a good and sufficient bond, to be approved by him, in a sum double the value of the property in the deed of trust, payable to the State of North Carolina, and conditioned that such trustee shall faithfully execute and carry into effect the provisions of said deed of trust. (1893, c. 453, s. 3; Rev., s. 969; C.S., s. 1613.)

§ 23-6. Trustee removed on petition of creditors; substitute appointed.

Upon the written petition of one-fourth of the number of the creditors of the grantor or assignor whose claims aggregate more than fifty per cent of the total indebtedness of said grantor or assignor, the clerk of the superior court of the county in which said deed of trust or deed of assignment is registered, upon a notice of not more than ten days to said trustee of said petition, shall remove said trustee and appoint some competent person to execute the provisions of such deed of trust or deed of assignment. (1909, c. 918, s. 3; C.S., s. 1614.)

§ 23-7. Substituted trustee to give bond.

Upon the removal or resignation of any trustee it is the duty of the clerk to require the person appointed to execute the provisions of such deed of trust, before entering upon his duties, to file with the clerk a good and sufficient bond, to be approved by him in a sum double the value of the property in said deed of trust, payable to the State of North Carolina, and conditioned that such person shall faithfully execute and carry into effect the provisions of said deed of trust. (1893, c. 453, s. 3; Rev., s. 970; 1909, c. 918, s. 4; 1915, c. 176, s. 2; C.S., s. 1615.)

§ 23-8. Only perishable property sold within ten days of registration.

27

It is unlawful for any trustee, whether named in such deed of trust or appointed by a clerk of the superior court, to sell any part of the property described in such deed of trust within ten days from the registration thereof, unless such property or some part thereof be perishable, in which case he may sell such property as is perishable, according to the powers conferred upon him in said deed of trust. (1893, c. 453, s. 4; Rev., s. 971; C.S., s. 1616.)

§ 23-9. Creditors to file verified claims with clerk; false swearing misdemeanor.

All creditors of the maker of such deed of trust shall, before receiving payment of any amount from the said trustee, file with the clerk of the superior court a statement under oath that the amount claimed by him is justly due, after allowing all credits and offsets, to the best of his knowledge and belief. Any creditor who shall knowingly swear falsely in such statement shall be guilty of a Class 1 misdemeanor. (1893, c. 453, ss. 6, 7; Rev., ss. 972, 3617; C.S., s. 1617; 1993, c. 539, s. 397; 1994, Ex. Sess., c. 14, s. 34, c. 24, s. 14(c).)

§ 23-10. Priority of payments by trustee.

The trustee, after paying the necessary costs of the administration of the trust, shall pay as speedily as possible

(1)   All debts which are a lien upon any of the trust property in his hands, to the extent of the net proceeds of the property upon which such debt is a lien;

(2)   Wages due to workmen, clerks, traveling or city salesmen, or servants, which have been earned within three months before registration of said deed of trust or deed of assignment, and

(3)   All other debts equally ratable. (1909, c. 918, s. 5; C.S., s. 1618.)

§ 23-11. Trustee to account quarterly; final account in twelve months.

The trustee, whether named in the deed of trust or appointed by a clerk of a superior court, shall within three months from the registration of such deed of trust, and at each succeeding period of three months, file with the clerk of the superior court of the county in which the same is registered an account under oath, stating in detail his receipts and disbursements and his action as trustee, and within twelve months he shall file his final account of his administration of his trust. The clerk may upon good cause shown extend the time within which the quarterly and final accounts herein provided for are to be filed. (1893, c. 453, s. 5; Rev., s. 973; C.S., s. 1619.)

§ 23-12. Trustee violating duties guilty of misdemeanor.

If any trustee in a deed of trust for the benefit of creditors shall fail to file his inventory as required by law, or shall knowingly make any false statement in such inventory, or shall knowingly fail to include any property therein, or shall sell any part of the property described in the deed of trust within ten days unless such property so sold be perishable, or shall fail to file either of the quarterly accounts or the final accounts as required by law, or shall knowingly make any false statement in such quarterly or final account, or shall knowingly fail to include any property, money or disbursement in such quarterly or final account, he shall, in either case, be guilty of a Class 1 misdemeanor. (1893, c. 453, s. 8; Rev., s. 3689; C.S., s. 1620; 1993, c. 539, s. 398; 1994, Ex. Sess., c. 24, s. 14(c).)

Article 2.

Petition of Insolvent for Assignment for Creditors.

§ 23-13. Petition; schedule; inventory; affidavit.

Every insolvent debtor may present a petition in the superior court, praying that his estate may be assigned for the benefit of all his creditors, and that his person may thereafter be exempt from arrest or imprisonment on account of any judgment previously rendered or of any debts previously contracted. On presenting such petition, every insolvent shall deliver therewith a schedule containing an account of his creditors and an inventory of his estate, which inventory shall contain -

29

(1)   A full and true account of his creditors, with the place of residence of each, if known, and the sum owing to each creditor, whether on written security, on account, or otherwise.

(2)   A full and true inventory of his estate, real and personal, with the encumbrances existing thereon, and all books, vouchers and securities relating thereto.

(3)   A full and true inventory of all property, real and personal, claimed by him as exempt from sale under execution.

He shall annex to his petition and schedule the following affidavit, which must be taken and subscribed by him before the clerk of the superior court, and must be certified by such officer:

I, _____, do swear (or affirm) that the account of my creditors, with the places of their residence, and the inventory of my estate, which are herewith delivered, are in all respects just and true; that I have not at any time or in any manner disposed of or made over any part of my estate for the future benefit of myself or my family, or in order to defraud any of my creditors; and that I have not paid, secured to be paid, or in any way compounded with any of my creditors, with a view that they, or any of them, should abstain or desist from opposing my discharge: so help me, God. (1868-9, c. 162, ss. 1, 2, 3; Code, ss. 2942, 2943, 2944; Rev., s. 1930; C.S., s. 1621.)

§ 23-14. Clerk to give notice of petition.

On receiving the petition, schedule and affidavit, the clerk of the superior court shall make an order requiring all the creditors of such insolvent to show cause before said officer, within thirty days after publication of the order, why the prayer of the petitioner should not be granted, and shall post a notice of the contents of the order at the courthouse door and three other public places in the county where the application is made for four successive weeks; or, in lieu thereof, shall publish the same for three successive weeks in any newspaper published in said county, or in an adjoining county. (1868-9, c. 162, ss. 4, 5; Code, ss. 2945, 2946; Rev., s. 1931; C.S., s. 1622.)

§ 23-15. Order of discharge and appointment of trustee.

If no creditor oppose the discharge of the insolvent, the clerk of the superior court before whom the hearing of the petition is had shall enter an order of discharge and appoint a trustee of all the estate of such insolvent. (1868-9, c. 162, s. 6; Code, s. 2947; Rev., s. 1932; C.S., s. 1623.)

§ 23-16. Terms and effect of order of discharge.

The order of discharge shall declare that the person of such insolvent shall forever thereafter be exempted from arrest or imprisonment on account of any judgment, or by reason of any debt due at the time of such order, or contracted for before that time, though payable afterwards. But no debt, demand, judgment or decree against any insolvent, discharged under this chapter, shall be affected or impaired by such discharge, but the same shall remain valid and effectual against all the property of such insolvent acquired after his discharge and the appointment of a trustee; and the lien of any judgment or decree upon the property of such insolvent shall not be in any manner affected by such discharge. (1868-9, c. 162, s. 9; Code, s. 2950; Rev., s. 1933; C.S., s. 1624.)

§ 23-17. Suggestion of fraud by opposing creditor.

Every creditor opposing the discharge of the insolvent may suggest fraud and set forth the particulars thereof in writing, verified by his oath; but the insolvent shall not be compelled to answer the suggestions of fraud in more than one case, though as many creditors as choose may make themselves parties to the issues in such cases. (1868-9, c. 162, s. 7; Code, s. 2948; Rev., s. 1934; C.S., s. 1625.)

Article 3.

Trustee for Estate of Debtor Imprisoned for Crime.

§ 23-18. Persons who may apply for trustee for imprisoned debtor.

When any debtor is imprisoned in the penitentiary for any term, or in a county jail for any term more than 12 months, application by petition may be made by any creditor, the debtor, or by his or her spouse, or any of his or her relatives, for the appointment of a trustee to take charge of the estate of such debtor. (1868-9, c. 162, s. 40; Code, s. 2974; Rev., s. 1943; C.S., s. 1626; 1977, c. 549.)

§ 23-19. Superior court appoints; copy of sentence to be produced.

The application must be made to the superior court of the county where the debtor was convicted, and upon producing a copy of the sentence of such debtor, duly certified by the clerk of the court, together with an affidavit of the applicant that such debtor is actually imprisoned under such sentence, and is indebted in any sum, the clerk or the judge may immediately appoint a trustee of the estate of such debtor. (1868-9, c. 162, ss. 41, 42; Code, s. 2975; Rev., s. 1944; C.S., s. 1627.)

§ 23-20. Duties of trustee; accounting; oath.

The trustee of the imprisoned debtor shall pay his debts pro rata. After paying such debts, the trustee shall apply the surplus, from time to time, to the support of the wife and children of the debtor, under the direction of the superior court. When the imprisoned debtor is lawfully discharged from his imprisonment, the trustee shall deliver to him all the estate, real and personal, of such debtor, after retaining a sufficient sum to satisfy the expenses incurred in the execution of the trust and lawful commissions therefor. The trustee shall make his returns and have his accounts audited and settled by the clerk of the superior court of the county where the proceeding was had, in like manner as provided for personal representatives. Before proceeding to the discharge of his duty, the trustee shall take and subscribe an oath, well and truly to execute his trust according to his best skill and understanding. The oath must be filed with the clerk of the superior court. (1868-9, c. 162, ss. 43, 45, 46; Code, ss. 2976, 2978, 2979; Rev., ss. 1945, 1946, 1947; C.S., s. 1628.)

§ 23-21. Court may appoint several trustees.

The court has power, when deemed necessary, to appoint more than one person trustee under this chapter; but in reference to the rights, authorities and duties conferred herein, all such trustees shall be deemed one person in law. (1868-9, c. 162, s. 47; Code, s. 2980; Rev., s. 1948; C.S., s. 1629.)

§ 23-22. Court may remove trustee and appoint successor.

In case of the death, removal, resignation or other disability of a trustee, the court making the appointment may from time to time supply the vacancy; and all proceedings may be continued by the successor in office in like manner as in the first instance. (1868-9, c. 162, s. 48; Code, s. 2981; Rev., s. 1949; C.S., s. 1630.)

Article 4.

Discharge of Insolvent Debtors.

§ 23-23. Insolvent debtor's oath.

Prisoners in order to be entitled to discharge from imprisonment under the provisions of this article shall take the following oath:

I, _____, do solemnly swear (or affirm) that I have not the worth of fifty dollars in any worldly substance, in debts, money or otherwise whatsoever, and that I have not at any time since my imprisonment or before, directly or indirectly, sold or assigned, or otherwise disposed of, or made over in trust for myself or my family, any part of my real or personal estate, whereby to have or expect any benefit, or to defraud any of my creditors: so help me, God. (1773, c. 100, s. 1, P.R.; 1808, c. 746, s. 2, P.R.; 1810, cc. 797, 802, P.R.; 1830, c. 33; 1838, c. 23; 1840, cc. 33, 34; 1852, c. 49; R.C., c. 59, s. 1; 1868-9, c. 162, s. 31; 1881, c. 76; Code, s. 2972; Rev., s. 1918a; C.S., s. 1631.)

§ 23-24. Persons imprisoned for nonpayment of costs in criminal cases.

The following persons may be discharged from imprisonment upon complying with this article and G.S. 153-194:

Every person committed for the fine and costs of any criminal prosecution. (1773, c. 100, s. 1, P.R.; 1808, c. 746, s. 2, P.R.; 1810, cc. 797, 802, P.R.; 1830, c. 33; 1838, c. 23; 1840, cc. 33, 34; 1852, c. 49; R.C., c. 59, s. 1; 1868-9, c. 162, s. 26; Code, s. 2967; Rev., s. 1915; C.S., s. 1632; 1933, c. 228, s. 9.)

§ 23-25. Petition; before whom; notice; service.

Every such person, having remained in prison for 20 days, may apply by petition to the court where the judgment against him was entered, praying to be brought before such court at a time and place to be named in the petition, and to be discharged upon taking the oath hereinbefore prescribed. The applicant shall cause 10 days' notice of the time and place of filing the petition to be served on the sheriff or other officer by whom he was committed. In cases of conviction before a magistrate the clerk of the superior court of the county where the convicted person confined for costs is, may administer the oath and discharge the prisoner. (1773, c. 100, s. 1, P.R.; 1808, c. 746, s. 2, P.R.; 1810, cc. 797, 802, P.R.; 1830, c. 33; 1838, c. 23; 1840, cc. 33, 34; 1852, c. 49; R.C., c. 59, s. 1; 1868-9, c. 162, ss. 27, 28; 1873-4, c. 90; 1874-5, c. 11; Code, ss. 2968, 2969; 1891, c. 195; Rev., s. 1916; C.S., s. 1633; 1971, c. 1190, s. 1.)

§ 23-26. Warrant issued for prisoner.

The clerk of the superior court before whom such petition is presented shall forthwith issue a warrant to the sheriff, or keeper of the prison, requiring him to bring the prisoner before the court, at the time and place named for the hearing of the case, which warrant every such sheriff or keeper shall obey. (1773, c. 100, s. 1, P.R.; 1808, c. 746, s. 2, P.R.; 1810, cc. 797, 802, P.R.; 1830, c. 33; 1838, c. 23; 1840, cc. 33, 34; 1852, c. 49; R.C., c. 59, s. 1; 1868-9, c. 162, s. 29; Code, s. 2970; Rev., s. 1917; C.S., s. 1634; 1971, c. 1190, s. 2.)

§ 23-27. Proceeding on application.

At the hearing of the petition, if the prisoner has no visible estate, and takes and subscribes the oath or affirmation prescribed in this Article, the clerk of the superior court before whom he is brought, shall administer the oath or affirmation to him, and discharge him from imprisonment, of which an entry shall be made in the docket of the court. (1773, c. 100, s. 1, P.R.; 1808, c. 746, s. 2, P.R.; 1810, cc. 797, 802, P.R.; 1830, c. 33; 1838, c. 23; 1840, cc. 33, 34; 1852, c. 49; R.C., c. 59, s. 1; 1868-9, c. 162, s. 30; Code, s. 2971; Rev., s. 1918; C.S., s. 1635; 1971, c. 1190, s. 3.)

§ 23-28. Suggestion of fraud.

The chairman of the board of commissioners, and every officer interested in the fee bill taxed against such prisoner, may oppose his taking the insolvent debtor's oath above prescribed, and file particulars of the suggestion in writing, in the court where the same shall stand for trial as prescribed in this chapter in other cases of fraud or concealment. (1868-9, c. 162, s. 32; Code, s. 2973; Rev., s. 1919; C.S., s. 1636.)

§ 23-29. Persons taken in arrest and bail proceedings, or in execution.

The following persons also are entitled to the benefit of this article as hereinafter provided:

(1)   Every person taken or charged on any order of arrest for default of bail, or on surrender of bail in any action.

(2)   Every person taken or charged in execution of arrest for any debt or damages rendered in any action whatever. (1868-9, c. 162, s. 10; Code, s. 2951; Rev., s. 1920; C.S., s. 1637; 1967, c. 24, s. 5; c. 1078.)

§ 23-30. When petition may be filed.

Every person taken or charged as in the preceding section [§ 23-29] specified may, at any time after his arrest or imprisonment, petition the court from which the process issued on which he is arrested or imprisoned, for his discharge therefrom, on his compliance with this chapter. (R.C., c. 59, s. 3; 1868-9, c. 162, s. 11; Code, s. 2952; Rev., s. 1921; C.S., s. 1638.)

§ 23-30.1. Provisional release.

Every person who has filed a petition under the provisions of G.S. 23-30 shall be brought before a judge within 72 hours after filing the petition and shall be provisionally released from imprisonment unless a hearing shall be held and the creditor shall establish that the prisoner has fraudulently concealed assets. If, at the time he is brought before a judge, the prisoner makes a showing of indigency, counsel shall be appointed for the prisoner in accordance with rules adopted by the Office of Indigent Defense Services. A provisional release under this section shall not constitute a discharge of the debtor, and the creditor may oppose the discharge by suggesting fraud even if he has unsuccessfully attempted to oppose the provisional release on the basis of fraudulent concealment. The debtor may be provisionally released even though actual service upon the creditor has not been accomplished if 72 hours has passed since the debtor delivered the notice to the sheriff for service upon the creditor. (1977, c. 649, s. 5; 2000-144, s. 32; 2001-487, s. 13.)

§ 23-31. Petition; contents; verification.

The petition shall set forth cause of the imprisonment, with the writ or process and complaint on which the same is founded, and shall have annexed to it a just and true account of all his estate, real and personal, and of all charges affecting such estate, as they exist at the time of filing his petition, together with all deeds, securities, books or writings whatever relating to the estate and the charges thereon; and also what property, real and personal, the petitioner claims as exempt from sale under execution, and shall have annexed to it on oath or affirmation, subscribed by the petitioner and taken before any person authorized by law to administer oaths, to the effect following:

I, _____, the within named petitioner, do swear (or affirm) that the within petition and account of my estate, and of the charges thereon, are, in all respects, just and true; and that I have not at any time or in any manner disposed of or made over any part of my property, with a view to the future

36

benefit of myself or my family, or with an intent to injure or defraud any of my creditors: so help me, God. (R.C., c. 59, s. 3; 1868-9, c. 162, ss. 12, 13; Code, ss. 2953, 2954; Rev., s. 1922; C.S., s. 1639.)

§ 23-32. Notice; length of notice and to whom given.

Twenty days notice of the time and place at which the petition will be filed, together with a copy of such petition and the account annexed thereto, shall be personally served by such debtor on the creditor or creditors at whose suit he is arrested or imprisoned, and such other creditors as the debtor may choose, or their personal representatives or attorneys. If the person to be notified reside out of the State, and has no agent or attorney in the State, the notice may be served on the officer having the claim to collect, or by two weekly publications in any newspaper in the State. (1773, c. 100, s. 8, P.R.; R.C., c. 59, ss. 3, 20; 1868-9, c. 162, s. 14; Code, s. 2955; Rev., s. 1923; C.S., s. 1640.)

§ 23-33. Who may suggest fraud.

Every creditor upon whom the notice directed in G.S. 23-32 is served may suggest fraud upon the hearing of the petition, and the issues made up respecting the fraud shall stand for trial as in other cases. (1822, c. 1131, s. 4, P.R.; 1835, c. 12; R.C., c. 59, s. 13; 1868-9, c. 162, s. 15; Code, s. 2956; Rev., s. 1924; C.S., s. 1641.)

§ 23-34. Where no suggestion of fraud, discharge granted.

If no creditor suggests fraud or opposes the discharge of the debtor, the clerk of the superior court before whom the petition is heard shall forthwith discharge the debtor, and, if he surrenders any estate for the benefit of his creditors, shall appoint a trustee of such estate. The order of discharge and appointment shall be entered in the docket of the court. (1773, c. 100, P.R.; 1808, c. 746, s. 2, P.R.; 1810, cc. 797, 802, P.R.; 1830, c. 33; 1838, c. 23; 1840, cc. 33, 34; 1852, c. 49; R.C., c. 59, s. 1; 1868-9, c. 162, s. 16; Code, s. 2957; Rev., s. 1925; C.S., s. 1642; 1971, c. 1190, s. 4.)

§ 23-35. Continuance granted for cause.

When it appears to the court that any debtor, who may have given bond for his appearance under this chapter, is prevented from attending court by sickness or other sufficient cause, the case shall be continued to another day, or to the next term, when the same proceedings shall be had as if the debtor had appeared according to the condition of his bond, and in the event of his death in the meantime, his bond shall be discharged. (1822, c. 1131, s. 1, P.R.; R.C., c. 59, s. 10; 1868-9, c. 162, s. 18; Code, s. 2959; Rev., s. 1926; C.S., s. 1643.)

§ 23-36. Where fraud in issue, discharge only after trial.

After an issue of fraud or concealment is made up, the debtor shall not discharge himself as to the creditors in that issue, except by trial and verdict in the same, or by a discharge by consent. (R.C., c. 59, s. 17; 1868-9, c. 162, s. 21; Code, s. 2962; Rev., s. 1927; C.S., s. 1644.)

§ 23-37. If fraud found, debtor imprisoned.

If, on the trial, the jury finds that there is any fraud or concealment, the judgment shall be that the debtor be imprisoned until a full and fair disclosure and account of all his money, property or effects be made by the debtor. (1822, c. 1131, s. 4, P.R.; 1835, c. 12; R.C., c. 59, s. 14; 1868-9, c. 162, s. 20; Code, s. 2961; Rev., s. 1928; C.S., s. 1645.)

§ 23-38. Effect of order of discharge.

The order of discharge under the last four articles of this chapter, whether granted upon a nonsuggestion of fraud, upon the finding of a jury in favor of the debtor, or otherwise, shall be in like terms and have like effect as prescribed in G.S. 23-16; except that the body of such debtor shall be free from arrest or imprisonment at the suit of every creditor, and as to him only, to whom the notice required may have been given; and the notices, or copies thereof, shall in all cases be filed in the office of the superior court clerk. (1822, c. 1131, s. 4, P.R.; 1835, c. 12; R.C., c. 59, s. 11; 1868-9, c. 162, s. 19; Code, s. 2960; Rev., s. 1929; C.S., s. 1646.)

Article 5.

General Provisions under Articles 2, 3, and 4.

§ 23-39. Superior or district court tries issue of fraud.

In every case where an issue of fraud is made up as provided in this Chapter, the case shall be entered in the trial docket of the superior or district court, and stand for trial as other causes; and upon a finding by the jury in favor of the petitioner the judge shall discharge the debtor; if the finding is against the petitioner he shall be committed to jail until he makes full disclosure. (1868-9, c. 162, s. 8; Code, s. 2949; Rev., s. 1935; C.S., s. 1647; 1971, c. 1190, s. 5.)

§ 23-40. Insolvent released on giving bond.

Every debtor entitled under the provisions of this chapter to discharge as an insolvent may, at the time of filing his application for a discharge or at any time afterwards, tender to the sheriff or other officer having his body in charge, a bond, with sufficient surety, in double the amount of the sum due any creditor or creditors at whose suit he was taken or charged, conditioned for the appearance of such debtor before the court where his petition is filed, at the hearing thereof, and to stand to and abide by the final order or decree of the court in the case. If such bond be satisfactory to the sheriff, he shall forthwith release such debtor from custody. (R.C., c. 59, s. 27; 1868-9, c. 162, s. 17; Code, s. 2958; Rev., s. 1936; C.S., s. 1648.)

§ 23-41. Surety in bond may surrender principal.

The surety in any bond conditioned for the appearance of any person under this chapter may surrender the principal, or such principal may surrender himself, in discharge of the bond, to the sheriff or other officer of any court where such principal is bound to appear, in the manner provided in the chapter entitled Civil Procedure, article Arrest and Bail. (1793, c. 100, s. 7, P.R.; c. 380, s. 1, P.R.; 1822, c. 1131, s. 3, P.R.; R.C., c. 59, s. 23; 1868-9, c. 162, s. 22; Code, s. 2963; Rev., s. 1937; C.S., s. 1649.)

§ 23-42. Creditor liable for jail fees.

When any debtor is actually confined within the walls of a prison, on an order of arrest in default of bail or otherwise, the jailer must furnish him with necessary food during his confinement, if the prisoner requires it, for which the jailer shall have the same fees as for keeping other prisoners. If the debtor is unable to discharge such fees, the jailer may recover them from the party at whose instance the debtor was confined. And at any time after the arrest, the sheriff or jailer may give notice thereof to the plaintiff, his agent or attorney, and demand security of him for the prison fees that accrue after such notice, and if the plaintiff fails to give such security then the sheriff may discharge the debtor out of custody. (1773, c. 100, ss. 8, 9, P.R.; 1821, c. 1103, P.R.; R.C., c. 69, s. 5; 1868-9, c. 162, s. 24; Code, s. 2965; Rev., s. 1938; C.S., s. 1650.)

§ 23-43. False swearing; penalty.

If any insolvent or imprisoned debtor takes any oath prescribed in this chapter falsely and corruptly, that person is guilty of a Class I felony, and he shall never after have any of the benefits of this chapter, but may be sued and imprisoned as though he had never been discharged. (1793, c. 100, s. 10, P.R.; R.C., c. 59, s. 25; 1868-9, c. 162, s. 23; Code, s. 2964; Rev., ss. 1940, 3614; C.S., s. 1651; 1993, c. 539, s. 1263; 1994, Ex. Sess., c. 24, s. 14(c).)

§ 23-44. Powers of trustees hereunder.

Any trustee appointed under the last four articles of this chapter, as therein contemplated, is hereby declared a trustee of the estate of the debtor, in respect to whose property such trustee is appointed for the benefit of creditors, and is invested from the time of appointment with all the powers and authority, and subject to the control, obligations and responsibilities prescribed by law in relation to personal representatives over the estates of deceased persons; but all debts shall be paid by the trustees pro rata. (1773, c. 100, ss. 5, 6, P.R.; 1827, c. 44; 1830, c. 26, s. 2; R.C., c. 59, ss. 21, 22; 1868-9, c. 162, s. 44; Code, s. 2977; Rev., s. 1941; C.S., s. 1652.)

§ 23-45. Jail bounds.

Any imprisoned debtor may take the benefit of the prison bounds by giving security, as required by law, except as follows:

(1)   A debtor against whom an issue of fraud is found.

(2)   Any debtor who, for other cause, is adjudged to be imprisoned until he makes a full and fair disclosure or account of his property. (1818, c. 964, P.R.; R.C., c. 59, s. 27; 1868-9, c. 162, s. 25; Code, s. 2966; Rev., s. 1942; C.S., s. 1653.)

Article 6.

Practice in Insolvency and Certain Other Proceedings.

§ 23-46. Unlawful to solicit claims of creditors in proceedings.

It shall be unlawful for any individual, corporation, or firm or other association of persons, to solicit of any creditor any claim of such creditor in order that such individual, corporation, firm or association may represent such creditor or present or vote such claim, in any bankruptcy or insolvency proceeding, or in any action or proceeding for or growing out of the appointment of a receiver, or in any matter involving an assignment for the benefit of creditors. (1931, c. 208, s. 1.)

§ 23-47. Violation of preceding section a misdemeanor.

41

Any individual, corporation, or firm or other association of persons violating any provision of G.S. 23-46 shall be guilty of a Class 1 misdemeanor. (1931, c. 208, s. 3; 1993, c. 539, s. 399; 1994, Ex. Sess., c. 24, s. 14(c).)

Article 7.

Bankruptcy of Taxing, etc., Districts, Counties, Cities, Towns and Villages.

§ 23-48. Local units authorized to avail themselves of provisions of bankruptcy law.

With the approval of the Local Government Commission of North Carolina and with the consent of the holders of such percentage or percentages of its indebtedness as may be required by Public Act Number three hundred two of the Seventy-fifth Congress, First Session, entitled "An Act to amend an Act entitled 'An Act to establish a uniform system of bankruptcy throughout the United States' approved July first, one thousand eight hundred ninety-eight and Acts amendatory thereof and supplementary thereto," approved August sixteenth, one thousand nine hundred thirty-seven, as amended, any taxing district, local improvement district, school district, county, city, town or village in the State of North Carolina is authorized to avail itself of the provisions of said act of Congress as said act now exists or may be hereafter amended. (1939, c. 203.)

Chapter 24

Interest.

Article 1.

General Provisions.

§ 24-1. Legal rate is eight percent.

The legal rate of interest shall be eight percent (8%) per annum for such time as interest may accrue, and no more. (1876-7, c. 91; Code, s. 3835; 1895, c. 69; Rev., s. 1950; C.S., s. 2305; 1979, 2nd Sess., c. 1157, s. 1.)

§ 24-1.1. Contract rates and fees.

(a)   Except as otherwise provided in this Chapter or other applicable law, the parties to a loan, purchase money loan, advance, commitment for a loan or forbearance other than a credit card, open-end, or similar loan may contract in writing for the payment of interest not in excess of:

(1)   Where the principal amount is twenty-five thousand dollars ($25,000) or less, the rate set under subsection (c) of this section; or

(2)   Any rate agreed upon by the parties where the principal amount is more than twenty-five thousand dollars ($25,000).

(b)   As used in this section, interest shall not be deemed in excess of the rates provided where interest is computed monthly on the outstanding principal balance and is collected not more than 31 days in advance of its due date. Nothing in this section shall be construed to authorize the charging of interest on committed funds prior to the disbursement of said funds.

(c)   On the fifteenth day of each month, the Commissioner of Banks shall announce and publish the maximum rate of interest permitted by subdivision (1) of subsection (a) of this section on that date. Such rate shall be the latest published noncompetitive rate for U.S. Treasury bills with a six-month maturity as of the fifteenth day of the month plus six percent (6%), rounded upward or downward, as the case may be, to the nearest one-half of one percent (1/2 of 1%) or sixteen percent (16%), whichever is greater. If there is no nearest one-half of one percent (1/2 of 1%), the Commissioner shall round downward to the lower one-half of one percent (1/2 of 1%). The rate so announced shall be the maximum rate permitted for the term of loans made under this section during the following calendar month when the parties to such loans have agreed that the rate of interest to be charged by the lender and paid by the borrower shall not vary or be adjusted during the term of the loan. The parties to a loan made under this section may agree to a rate of interest which shall vary or be adjusted during the term of the loan in which case the maximum rate of interest permitted on such loans during a month during the term of the loan shall be the greater of the rate announced by the Commissioner in (i) the preceding calendar month or (ii) the calendar month preceding that in which the rate is varied or adjusted.

(d)   Any bank or savings institution organized under the law of North Carolina or of the United States may charge a party to a loan or extension of credit

43

governed by this section a fee for the modification, renewal, extension, or amendment of any terms of the loan or extension of credit, such fee not to exceed the greater of one-quarter of one percent (1/4 of 1%) of the balance outstanding at the time of the modification, renewal, extension, or amendment of terms, or fifty dollars ($50.00).

(e)   Any bank or savings institution organized under the law of North Carolina or of the United States may charge a party to a loan or extension of credit not secured by real property governed by this section an origination fee not to exceed the greater of one-quarter of one percent (1/4 of 1%) of the outstanding balance or fifty dollars ($50.00).

(f)   This section shall not be construed to limit fees on loans or extensions of credit in excess of three hundred thousand dollars ($300,000). (1969, c. 1303, s. 1; 1977, c. 778, ss. 1, 3; c. 779, s. 1; 1979, c. 138, s. 1; 1981, c. 465, s. 1; c. 934, s. 1; 1985, c. 663, s. 1; 1991, c. 506, s. 2; 1998-119, s. 1; 1999-75, s. 1.)

§ 24-1.1A. Contract rates on home loans secured by first mortgages or first deeds of trust.

(a)   Notwithstanding any other provision of this Chapter, but subject to the provisions of G.S. 24-1.1E, parties to a home loan may contract in writing as follows:

(1)   Where the principal amount is ten thousand dollars ($10,000) or more the parties may contract for the payment of interest as agreed upon by the parties;

(2)   Where the principal amount is less than ten thousand dollars ($10,000) the parties may contract for the payment of interest as agreed upon by the parties, if the lender is either (i) approved as a mortgagee by the Secretary of Housing and Urban Development, the Federal Housing Administration, the Department of Veterans Affairs, a national mortgage association or any federal agency; or (ii) a local or foreign bank, savings and loan association or service corporation wholly owned by one or more savings and loan associations and permitted by law to make home loans, credit union or insurance company; or (iii) a State or federal agency;

44

(3)   Where the principal amount is less than ten thousand dollars ($10,000) and the lender is not a lender described in the preceding subdivision (2) the parties may contract for the payment of interest not in excess of sixteen percent (16%) per annum.

(4)   Notwithstanding any other provision of law, where the lender is an affiliate operating in the same office or subsidiary operating in the same office of a licensee under the North Carolina Consumer Finance Act, the lender may charge interest to be computed only on the following basis: monthly on the outstanding principal balance at a rate not to exceed the rate provided in this subdivision.

On the fifteenth day of each month, the Commissioner of Banks shall announce and publish the maximum rate of interest permitted by this subdivision. Such rate shall be the latest published noncompetitive rate for U.S. Treasury bills with a six-month maturity as of the fifteenth day of the month plus six percent (6%), rounded upward or downward, as the case may be, to the nearest one-half of one percent (1/2 of 1%) or fifteen percent (15%), whichever is greater. If there is no nearest one-half of one percent (1/2 of 1%), the Commissioner shall round downward to the lower one-half of one percent (1/2 of 1%). The rate so announced shall be the maximum rate permitted for the term of loans made under this section during the following calendar month when the parties to such loans have agreed that the rate of interest to be charged by the lender and paid by the borrower shall not vary or be adjusted during the term of the loan. The parties to a loan made under this section may agree to a rate of interest which shall vary or be adjusted during the term of the loan in which case the maximum rate of interest permitted on such loans during a month during the term of the loan shall be the rate announced by the Commissioner in the preceding calendar month.

An affiliate operating in the same office or subsidiary operating in the same office of a licensee under the North Carolina Consumer Finance Act may not make a home loan for a term in excess of six (6) months which provides for a balloon payment. For purposes of this subdivision, a balloon payment means any scheduled payment that is more than twice as large as the average of earlier scheduled payments. This subsection does not apply to equity lines of credit as defined in G.S. 45-81.

(a1)   Subject to federal requirements, when a natural person applies for a home loan primarily for personal, family, or household purposes, the lender shall comply with the provisions of this subsection.

(1)   Not later than the date of the home loan closing or three business days after the lender receives an application for a home loan, whichever is earlier, the lender shall deliver or mail to the applicant information and examples of amortization of home loans reflecting various terms in a form made available by the Commissioner of Banks. The Commissioner of Banks shall develop and make available to home loan lenders materials necessary to satisfy the provisions of this subsection.

(2)   Not later than three business days after the home loan closing, the lender shall deliver or mail to the borrower an amortization schedule for the borrower's home loan. Provided, however, that a lender shall not be required to provide an amortization schedule unless the loan is a fixed rate home loan that requires the borrower to make regularly scheduled periodic amortizing payments of principal and interest; and provided further that, with respect to a construction/permanent home loan, the amortization schedule must be provided only with respect to the permanent portion of the home loan during which amortization occurs.

(3)   If the home loan transaction involves more than one natural person, the lender may deliver or mail the materials required by this subsection to any one or more of such persons.

(4)   This subsection does not apply if the home loan applicant is not a natural person or if the home loan is for a purpose other than a personal, family, or household purpose.

(b)   Except as provided in subdivision (1) of this subsection, a lender and a borrower may agree on any terms as to the prepayment of a home loan.

(1)   No prepayment fees or penalties shall be contracted by the borrower and lender with respect to any home loan in which: (i) the principal amount borrowed is one hundred fifty thousand dollars ($150,000) or less, (ii) the borrower is a natural person, (iii) the debt is incurred by the borrower primarily for personal, family, or household purposes, and (iv) the loan is secured by a first mortgage or first deed of trust on real estate upon which there is located or there is to be located a structure or structures designed principally for occupancy of from one to four families which is or will be occupied by the borrower as the borrower's principal dwelling.

(2)   The limitations on prepayment fees and penalties contained in subdivision (b)(1) of this section shall not apply to the extent state law limitations on prepayment fees and penalties are preempted by federal law or regulation.

(c)   If the home loan is one described in subdivision (a)(1) or subdivision (a)(2) of this section, the lender may charge the borrower the following fees and charges in addition to interest and other fees and charges as permitted in this section and late payment charges as permitted in G.S. 24-10.1:

(1)   At or before loan closing, the lender may charge such of the following fees and charges as may be agreed upon by the parties notwithstanding the provisions of any State law, other than G.S. 24-1.1E, limiting the amount of such fees or charges:

a.   Loan application, origination, commitment, and interest rate lock fees;

a1.   Fees to administer a construction loan or a construction/permanent loan, including inspection fees and loan conversion fees;

b.   Discount points, but only to the extent the discount points are paid for the purpose of reducing, and in fact result in a bona fide reduction of the interest rate or time-price differential;

c.   Assumption fees to the extent permitted by G.S. 24-10(d);

d.   Appraisal fees to the extent permitted by G.S. 24-10(h);

e.   Fees and charges to the extent permitted by G.S. 24-8(d); and

f.   Additional fees and charges, however individually or collectively denominated, payable to the lender which, in the aggregate, do not exceed the greater of (i) one quarter of one percent (1/4 of 1%) of the principal amount of the loan, or (ii) one hundred fifty dollars ($150.00).

(2)   Except as provided in subsection (g) of this section with respect to the deferral of loan payments, upon modification, renewal, extension, or amendment of any of the terms of a home loan, the lender may charge such of the following fees and charges as may be agreed upon by the parties notwithstanding the provisions of any State law, other than G.S. 24-1.1E, limiting the amount of such fees or charges:

a.   Discount points, but only to the extent the discount points are paid for the purpose of reducing, and in fact result in a bona fide reduction of, the interest rate or time-price differential;

a1.   Fees which do not exceed one quarter of one percent (1/4 of 1%) of the principal amount of the loan if the principal amount of the loan is less than one hundred fifty thousand dollars ($150,000), or one percent of the principal amount of the loan if the principal amount of the loan is one hundred fifty thousand dollars ($150,000) or more, for the conversion of a variable interest rate loan to a fixed interest rate loan, of a fixed interest rate loan to a variable interest rate loan, of a closed-end loan to an open-end loan, or of an open-ended loan to a closed-end loan;

b.   Assumption fees to the extent permitted by G.S. 24-10(d);

c.   Appraisal fees to the extent permitted by G.S. 24-10(h);

d.   Fees and charges to the extent permitted by G.S. 24-8(d); and

e.   If no fees are charged under subdivision (c)(2)b. of this section, additional fees and charges, however individually or collectively denominated, payable to the lender which, in the aggregate, do not exceed the greater of (i) one quarter of one percent (1/4 of 1%) of the balance outstanding at the time of the modification, renewal, extension, or amendment of terms, or (ii) one hundred fifty dollars ($150.00). The fees and charges permitted by this sub-subdivision may be charged only pursuant to a written agreement which states the amount of the fee or charge and is made at the time of the specific modification, renewal, extension, or amendment, or at the time the specific modification, renewal, extension, or amendment is requested.

(c1)   No lender on home loans under subdivision (a)(3) of this section may charge or receive any interest, fees, charges, or discount points other than: (i) to the extent permitted by G.S. 24-8(d), sums for the payment of bona fide loan-related goods, products, and services provided or to be provided by third parties and sums for the payment of taxes, filing fees, recording fees, and other charges and fees, paid or to be paid to public officials; (ii) interest as permitted in subdivision (a)(3) of this section; and (iii) late payment charges to the extent permitted by G.S. 24-10.1.

(c2)   No lender on home loans under subdivision (a)(4) of this section may charge or receive any interest, fees, charges, or discount points other than: (i)

48

the fees described in G.S. 24-10; (ii) to the extent permitted by G.S. 24-8(d), sums for the payment of bona fide loan-related goods, products, and services provided or to be provided by third parties and sums for the payment of taxes, filing fees, recording fees, and other charges and fees, paid or to be paid to public officials; (iii) interest as permitted in subdivision (a)(4) of this section; and (iv) late payment charges to the extent permitted by G.S. 24-10.1.

(d)   The loans or investments regulated by G.S. 53C-5-3 shall not be subject to the provisions of this section.

(e)   The term "home loan" shall mean a loan, other than an open-end credit plan, where the principal amount is less than three hundred thousand dollars ($300,000) secured by a first mortgage or first deed of trust on real estate upon which there is located or there is to be located one or more single-family dwellings or dwelling units.

(f)   Any home loan obligation existing before June 13, 1977, shall be construed with regard to the law existing at the time the home loan or commitment to lend was made and this act shall only apply to home loans or loan commitments made from and after June 13, 1977; provided, however, that variable rate home loan obligations executed prior to April 3, 1974, which by their terms provide that the interest rate shall be decreased and may be increased in accordance with a stated cost of money formula or other index shall be enforceable according to the terms and tenor of said written obligations.

(g)   The parties to a home loan governed by subdivision (a)(1) or (2) of this section may contract to defer the payment of all or part of one or more unpaid installments and for payment of interest on deferred interest as agreed upon by the parties. The parties may agree that deferred interest may be added to the principal balance of the loan. This subsection shall not be construed to limit payment of interest upon interest in connection with other types of loans. Except as restricted by G.S. 24-1.1E, the lender may charge deferral fees as may be agreed upon by the parties to defer the payment of one or more unpaid installments. If the home loan is of a type described in subdivision (1) of this subsection, the deferral fees shall be subject to the limitations set forth in subdivision (2) of this subsection:

(1)   A home loan will be subject to the deferral fee limitations set forth in subdivision (2) of this subsection if:

a.   The borrower is a natural person;

49

b.   The debt is incurred by the borrower primarily for personal, family, or household purposes; and

c.   The loan is secured by a first mortgage or first deed of trust on real estate upon which there is located or there is to be located a structure or structures designed principally for occupancy of from one to four families which is or will be occupied by the borrower as the borrower's principal dwelling.

(2)   Deferral fees for home loans identified in subdivision (1) of this subsection shall be subject to the following limitations:

a.   Deferral fees may be charged only pursuant to an agreement which states the amount of the fee and is made at the time of the specific deferral or at the time the specific deferral is requested; provided, that if the agreement relates to an installment which is then past due for 15 days or more, the agreement must be in writing and signed by at least one of the borrowers. For purposes of this subdivision an agreement will be considered a signed writing if the lender receives from at least one of the borrowers a facsimile or computer-generated message confirming or otherwise accepting the agreement.

b.   Deferral fees may not exceed the greater of five percent (5%) of each installment deferred or fifty dollars ($50.00), multiplied by the number of complete months in the deferral period. A month shall be measured from the date an installment is due. The deferral period is that period during which no payment is required or made as measured from the date on which the deferred installment would otherwise have been due to the date the next installment is due under the terms of the note or the deferral agreement.

c.   If a deferral fee has once been imposed with respect to a particular installment, no deferral fee may be imposed with respect to any future payment which would have been timely and sufficient but for the previous deferral.

d.   If a deferral fee is charged pursuant to a deferral agreement, a late charge may be imposed with respect to the deferred payment only if the amount deferred is not paid when due under the terms of the deferral agreement and no new deferral agreement is entered into with respect to that installment.

e.   A lender may charge a deferral fee under this subsection for deferring the payment of all or part of one or more regularly scheduled payments, regardless of whether the deferral results in an extension of the loan maturity

50

date or the date a balloon payment is due. A modification or extension of the loan maturity date or the date a balloon payment is due which is not incident to the deferral of a regularly scheduled payment shall be considered a modification or extension subject to the provisions of subdivision (c)(2) of this section.

(h)   The parties to a home loan governed by subdivision (a)(1) or (2) of this section may agree in writing to a mortgage or deed of trust which provides that periodic payments may be graduated during parts of or over the entire term of the loan. The parties to such a loan may also agree in writing to a mortgage or deed of trust which provides that periodic disbursements of part of the loan proceeds may be made by the lender over a period of time agreed upon by the parties, or over a period of time agreed upon by the parties ending with the death of the borrower(s). Such mortgages or deeds of trust may include provisions for adding deferred interest to principal or otherwise providing for charging of interest on deferred interest as agreed upon by the parties. This subsection shall not be construed to limit other types of mortgages or deeds of trust or methods or plans of disbursement or repayment of loans that may be agreed upon by the parties.

(i)   Nothing in this section shall be construed to authorize or prohibit a lender, a borrower, or any other party to pay compensation to a mortgage broker or a mortgage banker for services provided by the mortgage broker or the mortgage banker in connection with a home loan. (1973, c. 1119, ss. 1, 2; 1975, c. 260, s. 1; 1977, c. 542, ss. 1, 2; 1979, c. 362; 1983, c. 126, s. 4; 1985, c. 154, s. 1; c. 381, ss. 1, 2; 1987, c. 444, ss. 1, 3, 4; c. 853, s. 4; 1989, c. 17, ss. 13, 14; 1999-332, s. 1; 2000-140, ss. 40(a), 40(b); 2001-340, s. 1; 2001-413, s. 9; 2001-487, s. 56; 2012-56, s. 6.)

§ 24-1.1B. Repealed by Session Laws 1979, c. 335.

§ 24-1.1C: Repealed by Session Laws 1998-119, s. 2.

§ 24-1.1D. Expired.

§ 24-1.1E. Restrictions and limitations on high-cost home loans.

(a)   Definitions. - The following definitions apply for the purposes of this section:

(1)   "Affiliate" means any company that controls, is controlled by, or is under common control with another company, as set forth in the Bank Holding Company Act of 1956 (12 U.S.C. § 1841 et seq.), as amended from time to time.

(2)   "Annual percentage rate" means the annual percentage rate for the loan calculated according to the provisions of the federal Truth-in-Lending Act (15 U.S.C. § 1601, et seq.), and the regulations promulgated thereunder by the Federal Reserve Board (as said Act and regulations are amended from time to time).

(3)   "Bona fide loan discount points" means loan discount points knowingly paid by the borrower for the purpose of reducing, and which in fact result in a bona fide reduction of, the interest rate or time-price differential applicable to the loan, provided the amount of the interest rate reduction purchased by the discount points is reasonably consistent with established industry norms and practices for secondary mortgage market transactions.

(4)   A "high-cost home loan" means a loan other than a reverse mortgage transaction in which:

a.   The principal amount of the loan (or, in the case of an open-end credit plan, the borrower's initial maximum credit limit) does not exceed the lesser of (i) the conforming loan size limit for a single-family dwelling as established from time to time by Fannie Mae, or (ii) three hundred thousand dollars ($300,000);

b.   The borrower is a natural person;

c.   The debt is incurred by the borrower primarily for personal, family, or household purposes;

d.   The loan is secured by either (i) a security interest in a manufactured home (as defined in G.S. 143-147(7)) which is or will be occupied by the borrower as the borrower's principal dwelling, or (ii) a mortgage or deed of trust on real estate upon which there is located or there is to be located a structure or structures designed principally for occupancy of from one to four families which is or will be occupied by the borrower as the borrower's principal dwelling; and

e.   The terms of the loan exceed one or more of the thresholds as defined in subdivision (6) of this section.

(4a)   "Mortgage broker" is as defined in G.S. 53-243.01.

(5)   "Points and fees" is defined as provided in this subdivision.

a.   The term includes all of the following:

1.   All items paid by a borrower at or before closing and that are required to be disclosed under sections 226.4(a) and 226.4(b) of Title 12 of the Code of Federal Regulations, as amended from time to time, except interest or the time-price differential. However, the meaning of the term "points and fees" shall not include any up-front fees collected and paid to the Federal Housing Administration, the Veterans' Administration, or the U.S. Department of Agriculture to insure or guarantee a home loan.

2.   All charges paid by a borrower at or before closing and that are for items listed under section 226.4(c)(7) of Title 12 of the Code of Federal Regulations, as amended from time to time, but only if the lender receives direct or indirect compensation in connection with the charge or the charge is paid to an affiliate of the lender; otherwise, the charges are not included within the meaning of the phrase "points and fees".

3.   To the extent not otherwise included in sub-subdivision a.1. or a.2. of this subdivision, all compensation paid from any source to a mortgage broker, including compensation paid to a mortgage broker in a table-funded transaction. A bona fide sale of a loan in the secondary mortgage market shall not be considered a table-funded transaction, and a table-funded transaction shall not be considered a secondary market transaction.

4.   The maximum prepayment fees and penalties which may be charged or collected under the terms of the loan documents.

b.   Notwithstanding the remaining provisions of this subdivision, the term does not include (i) taxes, filing fees, recording and other charges and fees paid or to be paid to public officials for determining the existence of or for perfecting, releasing, or satisfying a security interest; and (ii) fees paid to a person other

53

than a lender or an affiliate of the lender or to the mortgage broker or an affiliate of the mortgage broker for the following: fees for tax payment services; fees for flood certification; fees for pest infestation and flood determinations; appraisal fees; fees for inspections performed prior to closing; credit reports; surveys; attorneys' fees (if the borrower has the right to select the attorney from an approved list or otherwise); notary fees; escrow charges, so long as not otherwise included under sub-subdivision a. of this subdivision; title insurance premiums; and premiums for insurance against loss or damage to property, including hazard insurance and flood insurance premiums, provided that the conditions in section 226.4(d)(2) of Title 12 of the Code of Federal Regulations are met.

c.   For open-end credit plans, the term includes those points and fees described in sub-subdivisions a.1. through a.3. of this subdivision, plus (i) the minimum additional fees the borrower would be required to pay to draw down an amount equal to the total loan amount, and (ii) the maximum prepayment fees and penalties which may be charged or collected under the terms of the loan documents.

(5a)   A "table-funded transaction" is a loan transaction closed by a mortgage broker in the mortgage broker's own name with funds advanced by a person other than the mortgage broker in which the loan is assigned contemporaneously or within one business day of the funding of the loan to the person that advanced the funds.

(6)   "Thresholds" means:

a.   Without regard to whether the loan transaction is or may be a "residential mortgage transaction" (as the term "residential mortgage transaction" is defined in section 226.2(a)(24) of Title 12 of the Code of Federal Regulations, as amended from time to time), the annual percentage rate of the loan at the time the loan is consummated is such that the loan is considered a "mortgage" under section 152 of the Home Ownership and Equity Protection Act of 1994 (Pub. Law 103-25, [15 U.S.C. § 1602(aa)]), as the same may be amended from time to time, and regulations adopted pursuant thereto by the Federal Reserve Board, including section 226.32 of Title 12 of the Code of Federal Regulations, as the same may be amended from time to time;

b.   The total points and fees, as defined in G.S. 24-1.1E(a)(5), exceed five percent (5%) of the total loan amount if the total loan amount is twenty thousand dollars ($20,000) or more, or (ii) the lesser of eight percent (8%) of the total loan amount or one thousand dollars ($1,000), if the total loan amount is less than twenty thousand dollars ($20,000); provided, the following discount points and prepayment fees and penalties shall be excluded from the calculation of the total points and fees payable by the borrower:

1.   Up to and including two bona fide loan discount points payable by the borrower in connection with the loan transaction, but only if the interest rate from which the loan's interest rate will be discounted does not exceed by more than one percentage point (1%) the required net yield for a 90-day standard mandatory delivery commitment for a reasonably comparable loan from either Fannie Mae or the Federal Home Loan Mortgage Corporation, whichever is greater;

2.   Up to and including one bona fide loan discount point payable by the borrower in connection with the loan transaction, but only if the interest rate from which the loan's interest rate will be discounted does not exceed by more than two percentage points (2%) the required net yield for a 90-day standard mandatory delivery commitment for a reasonably comparable loan from either Fannie Mae or the Federal Home Loan Mortgage Corporation, whichever is greater;

3.   For a closed-end loan, prepayment fees and penalties which may be charged or collected under the terms of the loan documents which do not exceed one percent (1%) of the amount prepaid, provided the loan documents do not permit the lender to charge or collect any prepayment fees or penalties more than 30 months after the loan closing;

4.   For an open-end credit plan, prepayment fees and penalties which may be charged or collected under the terms of the loan documents which do not exceed one percent (1%) of the amount prepaid, provided the loan documents do not permit the lender to charge or collect any prepayment fees or penalties more than (i) 30 months after the loan closing if the borrower has no right or option under the loan documents to repay all or any portion of the outstanding balance of the open-end credit plan at a fixed interest rate over a specified period of time or, (ii) if the borrower has a right or option under the loan documents to repay all or any portion of the outstanding balance of the open-end credit plan at a fixed interest rate over a specified period of time, 30 months after the date the borrower voluntarily exercises that right or option; or

c.   If the loan is a closed-end loan, the loan documents permit the lender to charge or collect prepayment fees or penalties more than 30 months after the loan closing or which exceed, in the aggregate, more than two percent (2%) of the amount prepaid. If the loan is an open-end credit plan, the loan documents permit the lender to charge or collect prepayment fees or penalties (i) more than 30 months after the loan closing if the borrower has no right or option under the loan documents to repay all or any portion of the outstanding balance of the open-end credit plan at a fixed interest rate over a specified period of time or, (ii) if the borrower has a right or option under the loan documents to repay all or any portion of the outstanding balance of the open-end credit plan at a fixed interest rate over a specified period of time, more than 30 months after the date the borrower voluntarily exercises that right or option, or (iii) which exceed, in the aggregate, more than two percent (2%) of the amount prepaid.

(7)   For a closed-end loan, "total loan amount" has the same meaning as the term "total loan amount" as used in section 226.32 of Title 12 of the Code of Federal Regulations, and shall be calculated in accordance with the Federal Reserve Board's Official Staff Commentary thereto. For an open-end credit plan, "total loan amount" means the borrower's initial maximum credit limit.

(b)   Limitations. - A high-cost home loan shall be subject to the following limitations:

(1)   No call provision. - No high-cost home loan may contain a provision which permits the lender, in its sole discretion, to accelerate the indebtedness. This provision does not apply when repayment of the loan has been accelerated by default, pursuant to a due-on-sale provision, or pursuant to some other provision of the loan documents unrelated to the payment schedule.

(2)   No balloon payment. - No high-cost home loan may contain a scheduled payment that is more than twice as large as the average of earlier scheduled payments. This provision does not apply when the payment schedule is adjusted to the seasonal or irregular income of the borrower.

(3)   No negative amortization. - No high-cost home loan may contain a payment schedule with regular periodic payments that cause the principal balance to increase.

(4)   No increased interest rate. - No high-cost home loan may contain a provision which increases the interest rate after default. This provision does not apply to interest rate changes in a variable rate loan otherwise consistent with the provisions of the loan documents, provided the change in the interest rate is not triggered by the event of default or the acceleration of the indebtedness.

(5) No advance payments. - No high-cost home loan may include terms under which more than two periodic payments required under the loan are consolidated and paid in advance from the loan proceeds provided to the borrower.

(6) No modification or deferral fees. - A lender may not charge a borrower any fees to modify, renew, extend, or amend a high-cost home loan or to defer any payment due under the terms of a high-cost home loan.

(c) Prohibited Acts and Practices. - The following acts and practices are prohibited in the making of a high-cost home loan:

(1) No lending without home-ownership counseling. - A lender may not make a high-cost home loan without first receiving certification from a counselor approved by the North Carolina Housing Finance Agency that the borrower has received counseling on the advisability of the loan transaction and the appropriate loan for the borrower.

(2) No lending without due regard to repayment ability. - As used in this subsection, the term "obligor" refers to each borrower, co-borrower, cosigner, or guarantor obligated to repay a loan. A lender may not make a high-cost home loan unless the lender reasonably believes at the time the loan is consummated that one or more of the obligors, when considered individually or collectively, will be able to make the scheduled payments to repay the obligation based upon a consideration of their current and expected income, current obligations, employment status, and other financial resources (other than the borrower's equity in the dwelling which secures repayment of the loan). An obligor shall be presumed to be able to make the scheduled payments to repay the obligation if, at the time the loan is consummated, the obligor's total monthly debts, including amounts owed under the loan, do not exceed fifty percent (50%) of the obligor's monthly gross income as verified by the credit application, the obligor's financial statement, a credit report, financial information provided to the lender by or on behalf of the obligor, or any other reasonable means; provided, no presumption of inability to make the scheduled payments to repay the obligation shall arise solely from the fact that, at the time the loan is consummated, the obligor's total monthly debts (including amounts owed under the loan) exceed fifty percent (50%) of the obligor's monthly gross income.

(3) No financing of fees or charges. - In making a high-cost home loan, a lender may not directly or indirectly finance:

57

a.   Any prepayment fees or penalties payable by the borrower in a refinancing transaction if the lender or an affiliate of the lender is the noteholder of the note being refinanced;

b.   Any points and fees; or

c.   Any other charges payable to third parties.

(4)   No benefit from refinancing existing high-cost home loan with new high-cost home loan. - A lender may not charge a borrower points and fees in connection with a high-cost home loan if the proceeds of the high-cost home loan are used to refinance an existing high-cost home loan held by the same lender as noteholder.

(5)   Restrictions on home-improvement contracts. - A lender may not pay a contractor under a home-improvement contract from the proceeds of a high-cost home loan other than (i) by an instrument payable to the borrower or jointly to the borrower and the contractor, or (ii) at the election of the borrower, through a third-party escrow agent in accordance with terms established in a written agreement signed by the borrower, the lender, and the contractor prior to the disbursement.

(6)   No shifting of liability. - A lender is prohibited from shifting any loss, liability, or claim of any kind to the closing agent or closing attorney for any violation of this section.

(d)   Unfair and Deceptive Acts or Practices. - Except as provided in subsection (e) of this section, the making of a high-cost home loan which violates any provisions of subsection (b) or (c) of this section is hereby declared usurious in violation of the provisions of this Chapter and unlawful as an unfair or deceptive act or practice in or affecting commerce in violation of the provisions of G.S. 75-1.1. The provisions of this section shall apply to any person who in bad faith attempts to avoid the application of this section by (i) the structuring of a loan transaction as an open-end credit plan for the purpose and with the intent of evading the provisions of this section when the loan would have been a high-cost home loan if the loan had been structured as a closed-end loan, or (ii) dividing any loan transaction into separate parts for the purpose and with the intent of evading the provisions of this section, or (iii) any other such subterfuge. The Attorney General, the Commissioner of Banks, or any party to a high-cost home loan may enforce the provisions of this section. Any person seeking damages or penalties under the provisions of this section may recover damages under either this Chapter or Chapter 75, but not both.

(e)   Corrections and Unintentional Violations. - A lender in a high-cost home loan who, when acting in good faith, fails to comply with subsections (b) or (c) of this section, will not be deemed to have violated this section if the lender establishes that either:

(1)   Within 30 days of the loan closing and prior to the institution of any action under this section, the borrower is notified of the compliance failure, appropriate restitution is made, and whatever adjustments are necessary are made to the loan to either, at the choice of the borrower, (i) make the high-cost home loan satisfy the requirements of subsections (b) and (c) of this section, or (ii) change the terms of the loan in a manner beneficial to the borrower so that the loan will no longer be considered a high-cost home loan subject to the provisions of this section; or

(2)   The compliance failure was not intentional and resulted from a bona fide error notwithstanding the maintenance of procedures reasonably adapted to avoid such errors, and within 60 days after the discovery of the compliance failure and prior to the institution of any action under this section or the receipt of written notice of the compliance failure, the borrower is notified of the compliance failure, appropriate restitution is made, and whatever adjustments are necessary are made to the loan to either, at the choice of the borrower, (i) make the high-cost home loan satisfy the requirements of subsections (b) and (c) of this section, or (ii) change the terms of the loan in a manner beneficial to the borrower so that the loan will no longer be considered a high-cost home loan subject to the provisions of this section. Examples of a bona fide error include clerical, calculation, computer malfunction and programming, and printing errors. An error of legal judgment with respect to a person's obligations under this section is not a bona fide error.

(f)   Severability. - The provisions of this section shall be severable, and if any phrase, clause, sentence, or provision is declared to be invalid or is preempted by federal law or regulation, the validity of the remainder of this section shall not be affected thereby. If any provision of this section is declared to be inapplicable to any specific category, type, or kind of points and fees, the provisions of this section shall nonetheless continue to apply with respect to all other points and fees.

(g) A mortgage broker who brokers a high-cost home loan that violates any provisions of subsection (b) or (c) of this section shall be jointly and severally liable with the lender. (1999-332, s. 2; 2000-140, s. 40.1; 2001-487, s. 14(a); 2003-401, s. 3; 2007-352, ss. 1-3; 2008-227, s. 2; 2008-228, s. 15; 2009-457, s. 1; 2010-168, ss. 7, 8; 2013-399, ss. 1, 2.)

§ 24-1.1F. Rate spread home loans.

(a) Repealed by Session Laws 2013-399, s. 3, effective October 1, 2013.

(a1) A rate spread home loan is a loan that has an annual percentage rate that exceeds the limits set out in 15 U.S.C. § 1639c(c)(1)(B)(ii) and any regulations promulgated thereunder.

(b) Repealed by Session Laws 2013-399, s. 3, effective October 1, 2013.

(b1) The making of a rate spread home loan that violates 15 U.S.C. § 1639c(a) and any regulations promulgated thereunder is hereby declared usurious in violation of the provisions of this Chapter.

(c) Repealed by Session Laws 2013-399, s. 3, effective October 1, 2013.

(c1) Any prepayment penalty in violation of 15 U.S.C. § 1639c(c) and any regulations promulgated thereunder shall be unenforceable.

(d) Repealed by Session Laws 2013-399, s. 3, effective October 1, 2013.

(d1) Notwithstanding the foregoing, a borrower shall not be entitled to recover twice for the same wrong. The Attorney General, the Commissioner of Banks, or any party to a rate spread home loan may enforce the provisions of this section. This section establishes specific consumer protections in rate spread home loans in addition to other consumer protections that may be otherwise available by law. A mortgage broker who brokers a rate spread home loan that violates the provisions of this section shall be jointly and severally liable with the lender.

(e) The provisions of this section shall apply to any person who in bad faith attempts to avoid the application of this section by (i) dividing any loan transaction into separate parts for the purpose and with the intent of evading the provisions of this section, or (ii) any other such subterfuge.

(f)   A lender in a rate spread home loan who, when acting in good faith, fails to comply with this section, will not be deemed to have violated this section if the lender establishes that either:

(1)   Within 90 days of the loan closing and prior to the institution of any action against the lender under this section, the borrower was notified of the compliance failure, the lender tendered appropriate restitution, the lender offered, at the borrower's option, either to (i) make the rate spread home loan comply with subsection (b) or (c), or (ii) change the terms of the loan in a manner beneficial to the borrower so that the loan will no longer be considered a rate spread home loan subject to the provisions of this section, and within a reasonable period of time following the borrower's election of remedies, the lender took appropriate action based on the borrower's choice; or

(2)   The compliance failure was not intentional and resulted from a bona fide error notwithstanding the maintenance of procedures reasonably adopted to avoid such errors, and within 120 days after the discovery of the compliance failure and prior to the institution of any action against the lender under this section or the lender's receipt of written notice of the compliance failure, the borrower was notified of the compliance failure, the lender tendered appropriate restitution, the lender offered, at the borrower's option, either to (i) make the rate spread home loan comply with subsection (b) or (c) of this section, or (ii) change the terms of the loan in a manner beneficial to the borrower so that the loan will no longer be considered a rate spread home loan subject to the provisions of this section, and within a reasonable period of time following the borrower's election of remedies, the lender took appropriate action based on the borrower's choice. Examples of a bona fide error include clerical, calculation, computer malfunction and programming, and printing errors. An error of legal judgment with respect to a person's obligations under this section is not a bona fide error.

(g)   The provisions of this section shall be severable, and if any phrase, clause, sentence, or provision is declared to be invalid or is preempted by federal law or regulation, the validity of the remainder of this section shall not be affected thereby. (2007-352, s. 4; 2008-228, s. 16; 2009-457, s. 2; 2013-399, s. 3.)

§ 24-1.2: Repealed by Session Laws 1998-119, s. 2.

§ 24-1.2A. Equity lines of credit.

(a)   Notwithstanding any other provision of this Chapter, the parties to an equity line of credit, as defined in G.S. 45-81, may contract in writing for interest at rates which shall not exceed the maximum rates permitted under G.S. 24-1.1(c); provided, however, that the parties may contract for interest rates which shall be adjustable or variable, so long as for adjustable or variable rate contracts the rate in effect for a given period does not exceed the maximum rate permitted under G.S. 24-1.1(c) for the same period.

(b)   Fees may be charged on equity lines of credit which in the aggregate, over the life of the contract based on the maximum limit of the line of credit, do not exceed those permitted under G.S. 24-10. Any lender may charge a party to a loan or extension of credit governed by this section a fee for the modification, renewal, extension, or amendment of any terms of the loan or extension of credit, such fee not to exceed the greater of one-quarter of one percent (1/4 of 1%) of the balance outstanding at the time of the modification, renewal, extension, or amendment of terms, or fifty dollars ($50.00). (1985, c. 207, s. 1; 1991, c. 506, s. 4; 1998-119, s. 2.1.)

§ 24-1.3: Repealed by Session Laws 1979, 2nd Session, c. 1302, s. 3.

§ 24-1.4. Interest rates for savings and loan associations.

(a)   Notwithstanding any other provision of law, a savings and loan association domiciled in North Carolina may charge interest or collect fees with respect to any loan to the same extent as if the provisions of section 501 of Public Laws 96-221, as interpreted by the Federal Home Loan Bank Board prior to the effective date of this section, were still in effect in North Carolina.

(b)   Notwithstanding any other provision of law, any savings and loan association in North Carolina may contract for interest on any loan, purchase money loan, advance, commitment for a loan or forbearance at any rate permitted by federal law to a savings and loan association the accounts of which are insured by the Federal Savings and Loan Insurance Corporation. (1981, c. 282, s. 3; 1983, c. 126, s. 6.)

§ 24-2. Penalty for usury; corporate bonds may be sold below par.

The taking, receiving, reserving or charging a greater rate of interest than permitted by this chapter or other applicable law, either before or after the interest may accrue, when knowingly done, shall be a forfeiture of the entire interest which the note or other evidence of debt carries with it, or which has been agreed to be paid thereon. And in case a greater rate of interest has been paid, the person or his legal representatives or corporation by whom it has been paid, may recover back twice the amount of interest paid in an action in the nature of action for debt. In any action brought in any court of competent jurisdiction to recover upon any such note or other evidence of debt, it is lawful for the party against whom the action is brought to plead as a counterclaim the penalty above provided for, to wit, twice the amount of interest paid as aforesaid, and also the forfeiture of the entire interest. If security has been given for an usurious loan and the debtor or other person having an interest in the security seeks relief against the enforcement of the security or seeks any other affirmative relief, the debtor or other person having an interest in the security shall not be required to pay or to offer to pay the principal plus legal interest as a condition to obtaining the relief sought but shall be entitled to the advantages provided in this section. Nothing contained in this section or in G.S. 24-1, however, shall be held or construed to prohibit private corporations from paying a commission on or for the sale of their coupon bonds, nor from selling such bonds for less than the par value thereof. (1876-7, c. 91; Code, s. 3836; 1895, c. 69; 1903, c. 154; Rev., s. 1951; C.S., s. 2306; 1955, c. 1196; 1959, c. 110; 1969, c. 1303, s. 3.)

§ 24-2.1. Transactions governed by Chapter.

(a)   For purposes of this Chapter, any extension of credit shall be deemed to have been made in this State, and therefore subject to the provisions of this Chapter if the lender offers or agrees in this State to lend to a borrower who is a resident of this State, or if such borrower accepts or makes the offer in this State to borrow, regardless of the situs of the contract as specified therein.

(b)   Any solicitation or communication to lend, oral or written, originating outside of this State, but forwarded to and received in this State by a borrower who is a resident of this State, shall be deemed to be an offer or agreement to lend in this State.

(c)   Any solicitation or communication to borrow, oral or written, originating within this State, from a borrower who is a resident of this State, but forwarded to, and received by a lender outside of this State, shall be deemed to be an acceptance or offer to borrow in this State.

(d)   Any oral or written offer, acceptance, solicitation or communication to lend or borrow, made in this State to, or received in this State from, a borrower who is not a resident of this State shall be subject to the provisions of this Chapter, applicable federal law, law of the situs of the contract, or law of the residence of any such borrower as the parties may elect.

(e)   Any person who acquires a right by contract or by assignment to receive payments under a loan made in this State to an individual or individuals who is a resident of this State at the time of the loan and who benefits from the laws of this State by having the loan secured by real property located in this State is deemed to have consented to the courts of this State having jurisdiction over such person for any claim under this Chapter and for any claim related to the loan instrument.

(f)   The provisions of this section shall be severable and if any phrase, clause, sentence or provision is declared to be invalid, the validity of the remainder of this section shall not be affected thereby.

(g)   It is the paramount public policy of North Carolina to protect North Carolina resident borrowers through the application of North Carolina interest laws. Any provision of this section which acts to interfere in the attainment of that public policy shall be of no effect. (1979, c. 706, s. 3; 1983, c. 126, s. 11; 2007-351, s. 3.)

§ 24-2.2. Interest on extensions of credit by banks and savings and loan associations; exceptions.

Notwithstanding any other provision of law, banks and savings and loan associations chartered in North Carolina by the State of North Carolina or the federal government shall each be entitled to charge on extensions of credit those interest rates allowed any lender under North Carolina law. Provided, that any extension of credit pursuant to this authority shall be governed by those restrictions or limitations contained in the authorizing statute. Provided further, the authority granted under this section shall not apply to rates provided in Article 15 of Chapter 53, the Consumer Finance Act, nor in Subchapter III of Chapter 54, concerning credit unions. (1983, c. 126, s. 8.)

§ 24-2.3. State opt-out from federal preemption.

(a)   The provisions of section 501, of United States Public Law 96-221, as well as any modifications made to date, shall not apply to loans, mortgages, credit sales and advances made in this State.

(b)   Effective July 1, 1995, sections 521-524 of United States Public Law 96-221, shall apply to loans, mortgages, credit sales, and advances made in this State on or after that date as if North Carolina had never opted out of sections 521-524 of United States Public Law 96-221. (1983, c. 126, s. 1; 1995, c. 387, s. 1.)

§ 24-2.4. Prepayment of a loan if there are no prepayment terms or if the prepayment terms are not in accordance with law.

A borrower may prepay a loan in whole or in part without penalty where the loan instrument does not explicitly state the borrower's rights with respect to prepayment or where the provisions for prepayment are not in accordance with law. (1985, c. 681, s. 1.)

§ 24-2.5. Mortgage bankers and mortgage brokers.

A mortgage broker or a mortgage banker originating a loan in a table-funded loan transaction in which the mortgage broker or mortgage banker is identified as the original payee of the note shall be considered a lender for purposes of this Chapter. (1999-332, s. 3.)

§ 24-3. Time from which interest runs.

Interest is due and payable on instruments, as follows:

(1)   All bonds, bills, notes, bills of exchange, liquidated and settled accounts shall bear interest from the time they become due, provided such liquidated and settled accounts be signed by the debtor, unless it is specially expressed that interest is not to accrue until a time mentioned in the said writings or securities.

(2)   All bills, bonds, or notes payable on demand shall be held and deemed to be due when demandable by the creditor, and shall bear interest from the time they are demandable, unless otherwise expressed.

(3)   All securities for the payment or delivery of specific articles shall bear interest as moneyed contracts; and the articles shall be rated by the jury at the time they become due.

(4)   Bills of exchange drawn or indorsed in the State, and which have been protested, shall carry interest, not from the date thereof, but from the time of payment therein mentioned. (1786, c. 248, P.R.; 1828, c. 2; R.C., c. 13; Code, ss. 44, 45, 46, 47; Rev., s. 1952; C.S., s. 2307.)

§ 24-4. Obligations due guardians to bear compound interest; rate of interest.

Guardians shall have power to lend any portion of the estate of their wards upon bond with sufficient security, to be repaid with interest annually, and all the bonds, notes or other obligations which he shall take as guardian shall bear compound interest, for which he must account, and he may assign the same to the ward on settlement with him. On loans made out of the estate of their wards, guardians may lend at any rate of interest not less than four percent per annum and not more than the maximum lawful rate. This section shall in no way limit or affect the powers of guardians to make other investments which are now or may hereafter be authorized or permitted by the laws, statutory or otherwise, of the State of North Carolina. (1762, c. 69, P.R.; 1816, c. 925, P.R.; R.C., c. 54, s. 23; 1868-9, c. 201, s. 29; Code, s. 1592; Rev., s. 1953; C.S., s. 2308; 1943, c. 728; 1969, c. 1303, s. 4.)

§ 24-5. Interest on judgments.

(a)   Actions on Contracts. - In an action for breach of contract, except an action on a penal bond, the amount awarded on the contract bears interest from the date of breach. The fact finder in an action for breach of contract shall distinguish the principal from the interest in the award, and the judgment shall provide that the principal amount bears interest until the judgment is satisfied. If the parties have agreed in the contract that the contract rate shall apply after judgment, then interest on an award in a contract action shall be at the contract rate after judgment; otherwise it shall be at the legal rate. On awards in actions on contracts pursuant to which credit was extended for personal, family, household, or agricultural purposes, however, interest shall be at the lower of the legal rate or the contract rate. For purposes of this section, "after judgment" means after the date of entry of judgment under G.S. 1A-1, Rule 58.

(a1)   Actions on Penal Bonds. - In an action on a penal bond, the amount of the judgment, except the costs, shall bear interest at the legal rate from the date of entry of judgment under G.S. 1A-1, Rule 58, until the judgment is satisfied.

(b)   Other Actions. - In an action other than contract, any portion of a money judgment designated by the fact finder as compensatory damages bears interest from the date the action is commenced until the judgment is satisfied. Any other portion of a money judgment in an action other than contract, except the costs, bears interest from the date of entry of judgment under G.S. 1A-1, Rule 58, until the judgment is satisfied. Interest on an award in an action other than contract shall be at the legal rate. (1786, c. 253, P.R.; 1789, c. 314, s. 4, P.R.; 1807, c. 721, P.R.; R.C., c. 31, s. 90; Code, s. 530; Rev., s. 1954; C.S., s. 2309; 1981, c. 327, s. 1; 1985, c. 214, s. 1; 1987, c. 758; 1999-384, s. 1; 2000-133, s. 8; 2003-59, s. 4.)

§ 24-6. Clerk to ascertain interest upon default judgment on bond, covenant, bill, note or signed account.

When a suit is instituted on a single bond, a covenant for the payment of money, bill of exchange, promissory note, or a signed account, and the defendant does not plead to issue thereon, upon judgment, the clerk of the court shall ascertain the interest due by law, without a writ of inquiry, and the amount shall be

67

included in the final judgment of the court as damages, which judgment shall be rendered therein in the manner prescribed by § 24-5. (1797, c. 475, P.R.; R.C., c. 31, s. 91; Code, s. 531; Rev., s. 1956; C.S., s. 2310.)

§ 24-7. Interest from verdict to judgment added as costs.

Except with respect to compensatory damages in actions other than contract as provided in G.S. 24-5, when the judgment is for the recovery of money, interest from the time of the verdict or report until judgment is finally entered shall be computed by the clerk and added to the costs of the party entitled thereto. (Code, s. 529; Rev., s. 1955; C.S., s. 2311; 1981, c. 327, s. 2.)

§ 24-8. Loans not in excess of $300,000; what interest, fees and charges permitted.

(a)   If the principal amount of a loan is less than three hundred thousand dollars ($300,000), no lender shall charge or receive from any borrower or require in connection with any loan any borrower, directly or indirectly, to pay, deliver, transfer, or convey or otherwise confer upon or for the benefit of the lender or any other person, firm, or corporation any sum of money, thing of value, or other consideration other than that which is pledged as security or collateral to secure the repayment of the full principal of the loan, together with fees and interest provided for in this Chapter or Chapter 53 of the General Statutes.

(b)   Repealed by Session Laws 2003-401, s. 2, effective October 1, 2003, and applicable to contracts entered into or renewed on or after that date.

(c)   The provisions of this section shall not prevent a borrower from selling, transferring, or conveying property other than security or collateral to any person, firm, or corporation for a fair consideration so long as such transaction is not made a condition or requirement for any loan.

(d)   Notwithstanding any contrary provision of State law, any lender may collect money from the borrower for the payment of (i) bona fide loan-related goods, products, and services provided or to be provided by third parties, (ii) taxes, filing fees, recording fees, and other charges and fees paid or to be paid

68

to public officials, and (iii) fees payable to the federal government, any state or local government or any federal, state, or local governmental agency in connection with a loan made pursuant to a loan program sponsored by or offered through the federal government, any state or local government or any federal, state or local government agency, including loan guarantee and tax credit programs. No third party shall charge or receive (i) any unreasonable compensation for loan-related goods, products, and services, or (ii) any compensation for which no loan-related goods and products are provided or for which no or only nominal loan-related services are performed. Loan-related goods, products, and services include fees for tax payment services, fees for flood certification, fees for pest-infestation determinations, mortgage brokers' fees, appraisal fees, inspection fees, environmental assessment fees, fees for credit report services, assessments, costs of upkeep, surveys, attorneys' fees, notary fees, escrow charges, and insurance premiums (including, for example, fire, title, life, accident and health, disability, unemployment, flood, and mortgage insurance).

(e)   Notwithstanding any contrary provision of State law, any lender may receive the proceeds from any insurance policies where loss occurs under the terms of such policies.

(f)   This section shall not be applicable to any corporation licensed as a "Small Business Investment Company" under the provisions of the United States Code Annotated, Title 15, section 66, et seq., nor shall it be applicable to the sale or purchase of convertible debentures, nor to the sale or purchase of any debt security with accompanying warrants, nor to the sale or purchase of other securities through an organized securities exchange. (1961, c. 1142; 1969, c. 127; c. 1303, s. 5; 1993, c. 226, s. 12; 1999-332, s. 4; 2000-140, s. 40(c); 2003-401, s. 2.)

§ 24-9. Loans exempt from rate and fee limitations.

(a)   As used in this section, the following definitions apply:

(1)   "Bank" means a bank, savings and loan association, savings bank, or credit union chartered under the laws of North Carolina or the United States. However, the term "bank" does not include any subsidiary or affiliate of a bank, savings and loan association, savings bank, or credit union chartered under the laws of North Carolina or the United States that is not itself a bank, savings and

69

loan association, savings bank, or credit union chartered under the laws of North Carolina or the United States.

(2)   "Equity line of credit" means a loan, other than an exempt loan, that satisfies all of the following conditions:

a.   The lender is a bank.

b.   The loan is a revolving line of credit, open-end loan, revolving credit plan, or revolving credit card plan, and the loan is secured by a mortgage or deed of trust on real property.

c.   At any time within a specified period not to exceed 30 years the borrower may request and the lender is obligated to provide credit advances up to the agreed aggregate credit limit. As used in this sub-subdivision, "lender is obligated" means that the lender is contractually bound to provide credit advances. However, the equity line of credit and the lender's obligation to make credit advances shall be subject to the provisions of section 226.5b(f) of Title 12 of the Code of Federal Regulations and the official commentaries and rulings issued pursuant thereto, as the same may be amended from time to time, without regard to whether that section of the Code of Federal Regulations would otherwise apply to the loan.

d.   Any repayments of principal by the borrower within the specified time will reduce the amount of advances counted against the aggregate credit limit.

e.   The initial loan amount is ten thousand dollars ($10,000) or more. On January 1, 2008, and on January 1 every five years thereafter, the minimum initial loan amount sufficient to qualify a loan closed on or after that date as an equity line of credit under this section shall be increased by one thousand dollars ($1,000). For example, a loan closed on or after January 1, 2008, but prior to January 1, 2013, shall not be considered an equity line of credit unless the initial loan amount is eleven thousand dollars ($11,000) or more, and a loan closed on or after January 1, 2013, but prior to January 1, 2018, shall not be considered an equity line of credit unless the initial loan amount is twelve thousand dollars ($12,000) or more.

An equity line of credit shall cease being an equity line of credit subject to the provisions of this section from and after the date the loan amount is reduced below the equity line of credit's initial loan amount unless (i) the loan amount was reduced for one or more of the reasons or pursuant to one or more of the methods specified in section 226.5b(f)(2) or section 226.5b(f)(3)(vi) of Title 12 of the Code of Federal Regulations and the official commentaries and rulings issued pursuant thereto, as the same may be amended from time to time, without regard to whether that section of the Code of Federal Regulations would otherwise apply to the loan, or (ii) the loan amount was reduced at the request of the borrower because the borrower was engaged in the refinancing of a loan secured by a superior lien on the same real property and the reduction in the loan amount of the equity line of credit is no greater than the difference between the loan amount secured by the refinancing mortgage and the outstanding principle balance of the loan being refinanced.

(3)   "Exempt loan" means a loan in which:

a.   The loan amount is three hundred thousand dollars ($300,000) or more; or

b.   The borrower is a person other than a natural person; or

c.   The loan is obtained by a natural person primarily for a purpose other than a personal, family, or household purpose. Whether a loan is obtained primarily for a purpose other than a personal, family, or household purpose shall be guided by the standards established by the federal Truth In Lending Act (Title 1 of Public Law 90-321; 82 Stat. 146; 15 U.S.C. § 160, et seq.) and all regulations and rulings issued pursuant to that Act, as the same may be amended from time to time.

(4)   "Loan" means an advance of money or an extension of credit that is made to or on behalf of a borrower, the principal amount of which the borrower has an obligation to pay the lender. The term includes revolving lines of credit, open-end loans, revolving credit plans, and revolving credit card plans in addition to closed-end loans.

(5)   "Loan amount" means the principal amount of a loan or, in the case of a revolving line of credit, open-end loan, revolving credit plan, or revolving credit card plan, the initial maximum credit limit.

(b)   Notwithstanding any other provision of this Chapter or any other provision of State law, any borrower in an exempt loan transaction may agree to pay, and any lender, including a bank, may charge and collect from the borrower, interest at any rate and fees and other charges in any amount that the

71

borrower agrees to pay. A claim or defense of usury is prohibited in an exempt loan transaction.

(c)   The provisions of G.S. 24-1.2A, 24-11, and 24-11.1 shall not apply to equity lines of credit offered by banks. Except as provided in this subsection and notwithstanding any other provision of this Chapter or any other provision of State law, any bank may charge and collect from any borrower interest at any rate and fees and other charges in any amount that the borrower agrees to pay in connection with an equity line of credit. However, an equity line of credit made by a bank shall be subject to the following, to the extent otherwise applicable:

(1)   The provisions of G.S. 24-1.1E (relating to restrictions and limitations on high-cost home loans).

(2)   The provisions of G.S. 24-10.2 (relating to consumer protections in certain home loans).

(3)   Notwithstanding the limitation against prepayment penalties contained in G.S. 45-82.4, a bank may charge and collect prepayment fees or penalties following the borrower's voluntary exercise of a right or option to repay all or any portion of the outstanding balance of a variable interest rate equity line of credit at a fixed interest rate over a specified period of time, subject to the following limitations:

a.   Prepayment fees or penalties may be charged only with respect to the prepayment of that portion of the outstanding balance the borrower voluntarily agrees to repay at a fixed interest rate over a specified time;

b.   No prepayment fees or penalties may be charged for prepayments made more than 30 months after the borrower voluntarily exercises the right or option to repay that portion of the outstanding balance of the equity line of credit at a fixed interest rate over a specified period of time; and

c.   The prepayment fees or penalties charged with respect to that portion of the outstanding balance to be repaid at a fixed rate over a specified period of time may not exceed, in the aggregate, more than two percent (2%) of the amount prepaid.

Otherwise, no prepayment fees or penalties may be charged or collected by the bank with respect to an equity line of credit.

(d)   The provisions of G.S. 24-11 and G.S. 24-11.1 shall not apply to revolving credit card plans offered by banks. Notwithstanding any other provision of this Chapter or any other provision of State law, any bank may charge and collect from any borrower interest at any rate, as well as fees and other charges in any amount that the borrower agrees to pay in connection with a revolving credit card plan. This subsection (d) shall not apply to a revolving credit card plan that is secured by a mortgage or deed of trust on real property. (1963, c. 753, s. 1; 1965, c. 335; 1969, c. 896; 1979, c. 138, s. 5; 1995, c. 351, s. 13; 2003-401, s. 1; 2011-312, s. 1.)

§ 24-9.1. Certain repayments to consumers by public utilities not subject to claim or defense of usury.

Notwithstanding any other provision of this Chapter or any other provision of law, any public utility, as defined by G.S. 62-3, shall pay to its customers such rate of interest as may be required by order of the North Carolina Utilities Commission in transactions wherein the utility is refunding to its customers funds advanced by or overcollected from the customers. As to such transactions, the claim or defense of usury by such public utility and its successors or anyone else in its behalf is prohibited. (1981, c. 461, s. 3.)

§ 24-9.2: Repealed by Session Laws 1995, c. 351, s. 14.

§ 24-9.3. Economic development loans.

Fees or other funds paid by borrowers for contribution to loss reserve accounts administered and controlled by nonprofit corporations that are part of State-funded programs that provide loans to promote economic development shall not be considered interest under this Chapter and shall not be subject to claims or defenses of usury. (1995, c. 252, s. 1.)

§ 24-10. Maximum fees on loans secured by real property.

(a)   No lender on loans made under G.S. 24-1.1 shall charge or receive from any borrower or any agent for a borrower, any fees or discounts unless otherwise allowed where the principal amount is less than three hundred thousand dollars ($300,000) and is secured by real property, which fees or discounts in the aggregate shall exceed two percent (2%) if a construction loan on other than a one or two family dwelling, and one percent (1%) on any other type of loan; provided, however, if a single lender makes both the construction loan and a permanent loan utilizing one note, the lender may collect the fees as if they were two separate loans. Except as provided herein or otherwise allowed, no party shall pay for the benefit of the lender any other fees or discounts.

(b)   Any loan made under G.S. 24-1.1 in an original principal amount of one hundred thousand dollars ($100,000.00) or less may be prepaid in part or in full, after 30 days notice to the lender, with a maximum prepayment fee of two percent (2%) of the outstanding balance at any time within three years after the first payment of principal and thereafter there shall be no prepayment fee, provided that there shall be no prepayment fee charged or received in connection with any repayment of a construction loan; and except as herein provided, any lender and any borrower may agree on any terms as to prepayment of a loan.

(c)   "Construction loan" means a loan which is obtained for the purpose of financing fully, or in part, the cost of constructing buildings or other improvements upon real property and the proceeds of which, under the terms of a written contract between a lender and a borrower, are to be disbursed periodically as such construction work progresses; and such loan shall be payable in full not later than 18 months in case of a loan made under the provisions of G.S. 24-1.1(1) or 36 months in case of any other construction loan made after the execution of the note by the borrower. A construction loan may include advances for the purchase price of the property upon which such improvements are to be constructed.

(d)   (1)   Any lender may charge to any person, firm or corporation that assumes a loan, secured by real property, the following fee:

a.   Where the mortgage or deed of trust contains a due on sale clause, a fee not to exceed four hundred dollars ($400.00); provided, however, that if the original obligor is not released from liability on the obligation, the fee shall not exceed one hundred twenty-five dollars ($125.00).

74

b.   Where the mortgage or deed of trust does not contain a due on sale clause, a fee not to exceed one hundred twenty-five dollars ($125.00).

The fees authorized by this subsection may be paid in whole or in part by any party but the total shall not exceed the maximum fees set forth herein.

(2)   For purposes of this subsection, the term "due on sale clause" means a contract provision that authorizes a lender to declare immediately due and payable all sums secured by the lender's security instrument if all or any part of the secured property, or an interest therein, is sold or transferred without the lender's prior written consent or contrary to the requirements of the mortgage or the deed of trust. For purposes of this subsection, no lender shall exercise its rights under the due on sale clause if prohibited by federal law as of the date of execution of the contract containing the clause.

(e), (f) Repealed by Session Laws 1985, c. 755, s. 2.

(g)   Notwithstanding the limitations contained in subsection (a) of this section, a lender described in G.S. 24-1.1A(a)(2) may charge or receive from any borrower or any agent for a borrower, fees or discounts which in the aggregate do not exceed two percent (2%) on loans made under G.S. 24-1.1 or G.S. 24-1.2(2) when such loans are secured by a second or junior lien on real property. The fees or discounts are fully earned when the loan is made and are not a prepayment penalty under this Chapter or any other law of this State.

(h)   A bank, savings and loan association, savings bank, or credit union, or any subsidiary or affiliate thereof organized under the laws of this State or the United States, may charge a party to a loan secured by real property a reasonable fee as may be agreed upon by the parties for an appraisal performed by an employee of the bank, savings and loan association, savings bank, or credit union, or any subsidiary or affiliate thereof. Upon the request of the borrower, the lender shall provide at no additional charge to the borrower a copy of any appraisal for which the lender has collected a fee under this subsection. Provision of the copy of an appraisal shall not be construed to create or imply any warranty which does not otherwise exist by the lender as to the accuracy of the appraisal. (1967, c. 852, s. 1; 1969, c. 40; c. 1303, s. 6; 1971, c. 1168; 1979, c. 684; c. 849, s. 1; c. 969; 1981, c. 933; 1983, c. 541, s. 1; 1985, c. 154, s. 2; c. 755, s. 2; 1991, c. 506, s. 5.)

§ 24-10.1. Late fees.

(a)   Subject to the limitations contained in subsection (b) of this section, any lender may charge a party to a loan or extension of credit governed by the provisions of G.S. 24-1.1, 24-1.2, or 24-1.1A a late payment charge as agreed upon by the parties in the loan contract.

(b)   No lender may charge a late payment charge:

(1)   In excess of four percent (4%) of the amount of the payment past due; or

(2)   In excess of the amount disclosed with particularity to the borrower pursuant to the provisions of the Federal Consumer Credit Protection Act if the transaction is one to which the provisions of that act apply, which in no event shall exceed four percent (4%); or

(3)   For any payment unless past due for 15 days or more; provided, however, if the loan is one on which interest on each installment is paid in advance, no late payment charge may be charged until the payment is 30 days past due or more; or

(4)   More than once with respect to a single late payment. If a late payment charge is deducted from a payment made on the contract and such deduction results in a subsequent default on a subsequent payment, no late payment charge may be imposed for such default. If a late payment charge has been once imposed with respect to a particular late payment, no such charge shall be imposed with respect to any future payment which would have been timely and sufficient but for the previous default; provided that when a borrower fails to make an installment payment, and the terms of the loan agreement provide that subsequent payments shall first be applied to the past due balance, and the borrower resumes making installment payments but has not paid all past due installments, then the lender may enforce the contract according to its terms, imposing a separate late payment charge for each installment that becomes due until the default is cured; or

(5)   On any loan which by its terms calls for repayment of the entire balance in a single payment and not for installments of interest or principal and interest; or

(6)   Unless the lender notifies the borrower within 45 days following the date the payment was due that a late payment charge has been imposed for a particular late payment which late payment must be paid unless the borrower can show that the installment was paid in full and on time. No late payment charge may be collected from any borrower if the borrower informs the lender that non-payment of an installment is in dispute and presents proof of payment within 45 days of receipt of the lender's notice of the late charge.

(c)   The provisions of this subsection apply only to home loans made by lenders described in G.S. 24-1.1A(a)(2). Notwithstanding that the note or other loan document sets forth a late payment charge in excess of that permitted in this section, the loan shall not be deemed to be unlawful if:

(1)   No late fee in excess of those permitted in this section has been assessed or collected by the lender; and

(2)   a.   If the loan is executed on or after July 14, 1993, the lender provides written notice to the borrower within 90 days of the date of execution of the loan documents that the late payment charge with respect to the loan shall be four percent (4%) or less; or

b.   If the loan was executed prior to July 14, 1993, the lender provides written notice to the borrower within six months of that date that the late payment charge with respect to the loan shall be four percent (4%) or less. (1985, c. 755, s. 1; 1987, c. 447; 1993, c. 339, s. 1.)

§ 24-10.2. Consumer protections in certain home loans.

(a)   For purposes of this section, the term "consumer home loan" means a loan, including an open-end credit plan but excluding a reverse mortgage transaction, in which (i) the borrower is a natural person, (ii) the debt is incurred by the borrower primarily for personal, family, or household purposes, and (iii) the loan is secured by a mortgage or deed of trust upon real estate upon which there is located or there is to be located a structure or structures designed principally for occupancy of from one to four families which is or will be occupied by the borrower as the borrower's principal dwelling.

(b)   Notwithstanding the provisions of G.S. 58-57-35(b), it shall be unlawful for any lender in a consumer home loan to finance, directly or indirectly, any

77

credit life, disability, or unemployment insurance, or any other life or health insurance premiums; provided, that insurance premiums calculated and paid on a monthly basis shall not be considered financed by the lender.

(c)   No lender may knowingly or intentionally engage in the unfair act or practice of "flipping" a consumer home loan. "Flipping" a consumer loan is the making of a consumer home loan to a borrower which refinances an existing consumer home loan when the new loan does not have reasonable, tangible net benefit to the borrower considering all of the circumstances, including the terms of both the new and refinanced loans, the cost of the new loan, and the borrower's circumstances. This provision shall apply regardless of whether the interest rate, points, fees, and charges paid or payable by the borrower in connection with the refinancing exceed those thresholds specified in G.S. 24-1.1E(a)(6).

(d)   No lender shall recommend or encourage default on an existing loan or other debt prior to and in connection with the closing or planned closing of a consumer home loan that refinances all or any portion of such existing loan or debt.

(e)   The making of a consumer home loan which violates the provisions of this section is hereby declared usurious in violation of the provisions of this Chapter and unlawful as an unfair or deceptive act or practice in or affecting commerce in violation of the provisions of G.S. 75-1.1. The Attorney General, the Commissioner of Banks, or any party to a consumer home loan may enforce the provisions of this section. Any person seeking damages or penalties under the provisions of this section may recover damages under either this Chapter or Chapter 75, but not both.

(f)   In any suit instituted by a borrower who alleges that the defendant violated this section, the presiding judge may, in the judge's discretion, allow reasonable attorneys' fees to the attorney representing the prevailing party, such attorneys' fees to be taxed as a part of the court costs and payable by the losing party, upon a finding by the presiding judge that:

(1)   The party charged with the violation has willfully engaged in the act or practice, and there was unwarranted refusal by such party to fully resolve the matter which constitutes the basis of such suit; or

(2)   The party instituting the action knew, or should have known, that the action was frivolous and malicious.

(g)   This section establishes specific consumer protections in consumer home loans in addition to other consumer protections that may be otherwise available by law.

(h)   A mortgage broker who brokers a consumer home loan that violates the provisions of this section shall be jointly and severally liable with the lender. (1999-332, s. 5; 2003-401, s. 4; 2007-352, s. 5.)

§ 24-11. Certain revolving credit charges.

(a)   On the extension of credit under an open-end credit or similar plan (including revolving credit card plans, and revolving charge accounts, but excluding any loan made directly by a lender under a check loan, check credit or other such plan) under which no service charge shall be imposed upon the consumer or debtor if the account is paid in full within 25 days from the billing date, but upon which there may be imposed an annual charge not to exceed twenty-four dollars ($24.00), there may be charged and collected interest, finance charges or other fees at a rate in the aggregate not to exceed one and one-half percent (11/2%) per month computed on the unpaid portion of the balance of the previous month less payments or credit within the billing cycle or the average daily balance outstanding during the current billing period.

(a1)   If the lender chooses not to impose an annual charge under this section, the lender may impose a service charge not to exceed two dollars ($2.00) per month on the balance of any account which is not paid in full within 25 days from the billing date.

(a2)   No person, firm or corporation may charge a discount or fee in excess of six percent (6%) of the principal amount of the accounts acquired from or through any vendors or others providing services who participate in such plan.

(b)   On revolving credit loans (including check loans, check credit or other revolving credit plans whereby a bank, banking institution or other lending agency makes direct loans to a borrower), if agreed to in writing by the borrower, such lender may collect interest and service charges by application of a monthly periodic rate computed on the average daily balance outstanding during the billing period, such rate not to exceed one and one-half percent (11/2%).

79

(c)   Any extension of credit under an open-end or similar plan under which there is charged a monthly periodic rate greater than one and one-quarter percent (11/4%) may not be secured by real or personal property or any other thing of value, provided, that this subsection shall not apply to consumer credit sales regulated by Chapter 25A, the Retail Installment Sales Act; provided further, that in any action initiated for the possession of property in which a security interest has been taken, a judgment for the possession thereof shall be restricted to commercial units (as defined in G.S. 25-2-105(6)) for which the cash price was one hundred dollars ($100.00) or more.

(d)   The term "billing date" shall mean any date selected by the creditor and the bill for the balance of the account must be mailed to the customer at least 14 days prior to the date specified in the statement as being the date by which payment of the new balance must be made in order to avoid the imposition of any finance charge.

(d1)   A lender may charge a party to a loan or extension of credit governed by this section a late payment charge not to exceed five dollars ($5.00) on accounts having an outstanding balance of less than one hundred dollars ($100.00) and ten dollars ($10.00) on accounts having an outstanding balance of one hundred dollars ($100.00) or more, for any payment past due for 30 days or more; provided, in no case shall the late charge exceed the outstanding principal balance. If a late payment charge has been once imposed with respect to a late payment, no late charge shall be imposed with respect to any future payment which would have been timely and sufficient but for the previous default.

(e)   An annual or service charge pursuant to this section upon an existing credit card account upon which the charge has not previously been imposed may not be imposed unless the lender has given the cardholder at least 30 days notice of the proposed charge, and has advised the cardholder of his right not to accept the new charge. This notice shall be bold and conspicuous, and shall be on the face of the periodic billing statement or on a separate statement which is clearly noted on the face of the periodic billing statement provided to the cardholder. If the cardholder does not accept the new charge upon an existing credit card account, the lender may require that the cardholder make no further use of the account beyond the 30-day period in order to avoid paying the annual charge, but the cardholder shall be entitled to pay off any remaining balance according to the terms of the credit agreement. Nothing in this subsection shall limit the lender from decreasing any rates or fees to the cardholder forthwith.

Should any cardholder within 12 months of the initial imposition of an annual charge rescind his credit card contract and surrender all cards issued under the contract to the lender, he shall be entitled to a prorated refund of the annual fee previously charged, credited to the cardholder's credit card account. (1967, c. 852, s. 1.1; 1969, c. 1303, s. 7; 1977, c. 148, s. 1; cc. 917, 1108; 1979, 2nd Sess., c. 1330, s. 3; 1981, c. 844, s. 1; 1983, c. 126, ss. 5, 10; 1991, c. 506, s. 6; c. 761, s. 45; 1995, c. 387, s. 2; 2009-570, s. 27.)

§ 24-11.1. Disclosure requirements for credit cards.

(a)   This section applies to any application, solicitation of an application, offer of credit, or communication extending credit that is:

(1)   For an open-end credit plan accessed through a credit card or a revolving credit loan accessed through a credit card;

(2)   Printed;

(3)   Mailed or otherwise delivered to a person at any address within this State;

(4)   Not delivered pursuant to an existing credit agreement; and

(5)   Not printed in a newspaper, magazine, or periodical generally circulated outside as well as inside the State.

(b)   Disclosures. - The following disclosures shall be clearly and conspicuously made in or with all documents described in subsection (a) of this section:

(1)   The annual percentage rate or, if the rate may vary, a statement that it may vary, the circumstances under which the rate may increase, any limitations on the increase, and the effects of the increase on the other terms of the agreement.

(2)   The date or occasion upon which the finance charge begins to accrue on a transaction and the duration of any grace period.

(3)   Whether an annual fee is charged and the amount of the fee.

(4)   Any delinquency charge, late charge, or collection charge which may be assessed for the late payment of any installment, including the terms and conditions for the imposition of such charge.

(c)   Federal Requirements. - The form and content of the disclosures described in subsection (b) may be consistent with similar disclosures required by the federal Truth-in-Lending Act, 15 U.S.C. § 1601 et seq., and Regulation Z, 12 C.R.F. 226. Any amendment to the Act or Regulation that addresses credit card disclosures shall to the extent it covers applications, solicitations, and other communications covered by this section, replace the disclosure requirements of this section for creditors subject to the Act.

(d)   Penalty. - A violation of this section shall constitute a violation of G.S. 75-1.1 except that the creditor shall not be liable for any fine, civil penalty, treble damages, or attorney's fee where the creditor shows by a preponderance of the evidence that the violation was not intentional and resulted from a bona fide error, notwithstanding the maintenance of procedures reasonably adapted to avoid any such error.

(e)   Severability. - If any part of this section is found unconstitutional or is preempted by federal law with regard to a creditor because the creditor is located outside of the State, that part does not apply to creditors located within the State.

(f)   Nothing in this section shall be construed to authorize any fee, charge, surcharge or penalty not otherwise authorized by law. (1987, c. 735, s. 1.)

§ 24-11.2. Disclosure requirements for charge cards.

(a)   Applications and Other Communications. - This section applies to any application, solicitation of an application, offer of credit, or communication extending credit that is:

(1)   For credit accessed through a charge card;

(2)   Printed;

(3)   Mailed or otherwise delivered to a person at any address within this State;

(4)   Not delivered pursuant to an existing credit agreement; and

(5)   Not printed in a newspaper, magazine, or periodical generally circulated outside as well as inside the State.

For purposes of this section, the term "charge card" means any card, plate or other device pursuant to which the charge card issuer extends credit which is not subject to a finance charge and where the charge cardholder cannot automatically access credit that is repayable in installments.

(b)   Disclosures. - The following disclosures shall be clearly and conspicuously made in or with all documents described in subsection (a) of this section:

(1)   The annual fee and other charges, if any, applicable to the issuance or use of the charge card.

(2)   That charges incurred by the use of the charge card are due and payable upon receipt of a periodic statement of charges.

(3)   Any delinquency charge, late charge, or collection charge which may be assessed for late payment, including the terms and conditions for the imposition of such charge.

(c)   Federal Requirements. - The form and content of the disclosures described in subsection (b) may be consistent with similar disclosures required by the federal Truth-in-Lending Act, 15 U.S.C. § 1601 et seq., and Regulation Z, 12 C.F.R. 226. Any amendment to the Act or Regulation that addresses credit card disclosures shall, to the extent it covers applications, solicitations, and other communications covered by this section, replace the disclosure requirements of this section for creditors subject to the Act.

(d)   Penalty. - A violation of this section shall constitute a violation of G.S. 75-1.1 except that the creditor shall not be liable for any fine, civil penalty, treble damages, or attorney's fee where the creditor shows by a preponderance of the evidence that the violation was not intentional and resulted from a bona fide error, notwithstanding the maintenance of procedures reasonably adapted to avoid any such error.

83

(e)   Severability. - If any part of this section is found unconstitutional or is preempted by federal law with regard to a creditor because the creditor is located outside of the State, that part does not apply to creditors located within the State.

(f)   Nothing in this section shall be construed to authorize any fee, charge, surcharge or penalty not otherwise authorized by law. (1987, c. 735. s. 1.)

Article 2.

Loans Secured by Secondary or Junior Mortgages.

§ 24-12. Applicability of Article.

This Article shall apply only to loans of money:

(1)   Secured in whole or in part by a security instrument on real property, other than a first security instrument on real property; and

(2)   The principal amount of the loan does not exceed twenty-five thousand dollars ($25,000);

(3)   The loan is repayable in no less than six nor more than 181 successive monthly payments, which payments shall be substantially equal in amount. (1971, c. 1229, s. 2; 1979, 2nd Sess., c. 1157, ss. 2, 3.)

§ 24-13. Principal amount defined.

The aggregate of the amount or value actually received at the time of the loan, plus the charges allowed by G.S. 24-14(b) (c) and (f); plus the sum of all existing indebtedness of the borrower paid on his behalf by the lender, shall be deemed the principal amount of the loan. (1971, c. 1229, s. 2; 1979, 2nd Sess., c. 1157, s. 4; 1985, c. 154, s. 3.)

§ 24-14. Limitations on charges and interest.

(a)   No person, copartnership, association, trust, corporation or other legal entity making loans under this Article may charge, take or receive, directly or indirectly, simple interest in excess of one and one-half percent (1 ½%) per month or an annual rate equivalent to the Federal Discount Rate plus five percent (5%), whichever is the greater, computed on the actual or average daily unpaid balance of the principal amount of the loan for the time actually outstanding. However, interest may not be compounded.

(b)   In addition to the interest permitted in subsection (a), the lender may include in the loan his actual expenses which are paid to third parties in connection with the loan. Such expenses shall be limited to those for: title examination, title insurance, appraisals, surveys, and recording fees or releasing fees to trustees or public officials, and only such insurance charges as permitted in subsection (c).

(c)   Evidence of hazard insurance may be required by the lender of the borrower. Credit life, credit accident and health, and credit unemployment insurance, or any of them, may be offered but not required; provided (i) that the borrower has indicated a desire to purchase such insurance by signing a statement to that effect, (ii) that the borrower is advised that he may acquire this insurance from any insurance carrier, (iii) that the borrower is aware that this insurance may be rescinded within 30 days after receipt of the policy or certificate, and (iv) that the borrower directs the lender to purchase the above insurance from the proceeds of his loan.

The rates for the herein described insurance shall not exceed the standard rates approved by the Commissioner of Insurance for such insurance. Proof of all insurance issued in connection with loans subject to this Article shall be furnished to the borrower within 10 days from the date of application therefor by said borrower.

(d)   No application fee or other charge shall be allowed in the event the loan is not consummated.

(e)   The borrower shall further have the right to anticipate payment of his debt in whole or in part at any time, without payment of interest penalty, or any other fee or charge for such prepayment.

(f) In addition to the interest permitted by subsection (a), the lender may include in the principal balance fees or discounts not exceeding two percent (2%) of the principal amount of the loan less the amount of any existing loan by that lender to be refinanced, modified or extended. The fees and discounts are fully earned when the loan is made and are not a prepayment penalty. (1971, c. 1229, s. 2; 1973, c. 1150; 1977, c. 698, ss. 1, 2; 1979, 2nd Sess., c. 1157, ss. 5, 6; 1981, c. 464, s. 4; 1985, c. 154, s. 4; 1993, c. 226, s. 13.)

§ 24-15: Repealed by Session Laws 1979, 2nd Session, c. 1157, s. 7.

§ 24-16. Itemized closing statements.

Any person, copartnership, association, trust, corporation, or any other legal entity making on its own behalf, or as agent, broker or in other representative capacity on behalf of any other person, copartnership, association, trust, corporation or any other legal entity, a loan or real property financing transaction within the regulatory authority of this Article, at the time of the closing shall furnish the debtor or borrower or grantor in the mortgage, deed of trust or any other security instrument, in addition to the disclosures required by federal law known as "Truth in Lending," a complete and itemized closing statement which shall show all disbursements of the loan proceeds and which shall total the principal amount of the loan or security transaction, and the said closing statement shall be signed by the lending agency or a representative of the lending agency, or a responsible officer in its behalf and a completed and signed additional copy retained in the files of the lending agency involved and available at all reasonable times to the borrower, the borrower's successor in interest to the security real property, or the authorized agent of the borrower or the borrower's successor, until such time as the security instrument shall be satisfied in full. Such closing statement shall contain the following language printed in a conspicuous manner:

"This loan is one regulated by the provisions of Chapter 24, Article 2 of the General Statutes of North Carolina entitled 'Loans Secured by Secondary or Junior Mortgages'." (1971, c. 1229, s. 2.)

§ 24-16.1. Loans exempt from §§ 24-12 to 24-17.

G.S. 24-12 to 24-17 shall not apply to loans made by banks, insurance companies, or their duly designated agents compensated directly by the lender, duly licensed credit unions, production credit associations authorized by the Farm Credit Act of 1933, or savings and loan associations authorized to do business in this State, or to loans made by any other lender licensed by, and under the supervision of, the Commissioner of Banks and the State Banking Commission, under the provisions of Chapter 53 of the General Statutes, or the Commissioner of Insurance, under the provisions of Chapter 58 of the General Statutes. Provided, any lender approved as a mortgagee by the Federal Housing Administration shall be entitled to make loans under this Article.

G.S. 24-12 to 24-17 shall not apply to a loan made under Article 1 of this Chapter. (1971, c. 1229, s. 2; 1983, c. 126, s. 9; 1985, c. 154, s. 5.)

§ 24-17. Misdemeanors.

A wilful or knowing violation of G.S. 24-12 through G.S. 24-16 is hereby made a Class 1 misdemeanor. (1971, c. 1229, s. 2; 1993, c. 539, s. 400; 1994, Ex. Sess., c. 24, s. 14(c).)

Vision Books Order Form

Fax Orders:	1-980-299-5965
Phone Orders:	1-704-898-0770
E-mail Orders:	www.visionbooks.org
Mail Orders:	Vision Books, LLC P.O. Box 42406 Charlotte, NC 28215

Shipp To:
Name_____
Address_____
City_____State_____Zip_____
Phone_____Fax_____
Email_____@_____

Bill To: We can bill a third party on your behalf.
Name_____
Address_____
City_____State_____Zip_____
Phone____(_____)_____Fax_____
Email_____@_____

Pamphlet Number ($15.00 Each)	Qty	Total Cost
_____	_____	_____
_____	_____	_____
_____	_____	_____
_____	_____	_____
_____	_____	_____
_____	_____	_____
_____	_____	_____
_____	_____	_____
Full Volume Set 1-92	92 Pamphlets	1,380.00

Free Shipping Shipping & Handling on Full Volume Orders
Add $1.00 Shipping & Handling per pamphlet $_____

Total Cost $_____

Thank You for Your Support. Management!

DID YOU ENJOY THIS BOOK?

Vision Books would like to hear from you! If you or someone you know has been falsely imprisoned, we would like to hear your story. If the 'North Carolina Criminal Law and Procedure' has had an effect in your life or if you have suggestions, we would like to hear from you. Send your letters to:

Vision Books, LLC
Attn: Staff Writers
P.O. Box 42406
Charlotte, NC 28215
Email: staff@visionbooks.org

Order Additional Copies:

Fax Orders: 1-980-299-5965

Phone Orders: 1-704-898-0770

E-mail Orders: www.visionbooks.org

Mail Orders: Vision Books, LLC
                         P.O. Box 42406
                         Charlotte, NC 28215

www.ingramcontent.com/pod-product-compliance
Lightning Source LLC
Chambersburg PA
CBHW071245170526
45165CB00003B/1253